MUIRHEAD LIBRARY OF PHILOSOPHY

An admirable statement of the aims of the Library of Philosophy was provided by the first editor, the late Professor J. H. Muirhead, in his description of the original programme printed in Erdmann's *History of Philosophy* under the date 1890. This was slightly modified in subsequent volumes to take the form of the following statement:

'The Muirhead Library of Philosophy was designed as a contribution to the History of Modern Philosophy under the heads: first of Different Schools of Thought—Sensationalist, Realist, Idealist, Intuitivist; secondly of different Subjects—Psychology, Ethics, Aesthetics, Political Philosophy, Theology. While much had been done in England in tracing the course of evolution in nature, history, economics, morals and religion, little had been done in tracing the development of thought on these subjects. Yet "the evolution of opinion is part of the whole evolution".

'By the co-operation of different writers in carrying out this plan it was hoped that a thoroughness and completeness of treatment, otherwise unattainable, might be secured. It was believed also that from writers mainly British and American fuller consideration of English Philosophy than it had hitherto received might be looked for. In the earlier series of books containing, among others, Bosanquet's *History of Aesthetic*, Pfleiderer's *Rational Theology since Kant*, Albee's *History of English Utilitarianism*, Bonar's *Philosophy and Political Economy*, Brett's *History of Psychology*, Ritchie's *Natural Rights*, these objects were to a large extent effected.

'In the meantime original work of a high order was being produced both in England and America by such writers as Bradley, Stout, Bertrand Russell, Baldwin, Urban, Montague, and others, and a new interest in foreign works, German, French and Italian, which had either become classical or were attracting public attention, had developed. The scope of the Library thus became extended into something more international, and it is entering on the fifth decade of its existence in the hope that it may contribute to that mutual understanding between countries which is so pressing a need of the present time.'

The need which Professor Muirhead stressed is not less pressing today, and few will deny that philosophy has much to do with enabling us to meet it, although no one, least of all Muirhead himself, would regard that as the sole, or even the main, object of philosophy. As Professor Muirhead continues to lend the distinction of his name to the Library of Philosophy it seemed not inappropriate to allow him to recall us to these aims in his own words. The emphasis on the history of thought also seemed to me very timely; and the number of important works promised for the Library in the very near future augur well for the continued fulfilment, in this and other ways, of the expectations of the original editor.

H. D. LEWIS

MUIRHEAD LIBRARY OF PHILOSOPHY

General Editor: H. D. Lewis

Professor of History and Philosophy of Religion in the University of London

Action by SIR MALCOLM KNOX

The Analysis of Mind by BERTRAND RUSSELL

Belief by H. H. PRICE

Brett's History of Psychology edited by R. S. PETERS

Clarity is Not Enough by H. D. LEWIS

Coleridge as a Philosopher by J. H. MUIRHEAD

The Commonplace Book of G. E. Moore edited by C. LEWY

Contemporary American Philosophy edited by G. P. ADAMS and W. P. MONTAGUE

Contemporary British Philosophy first and second Series edited by J. H. MUIRHEAD

Contemporary British Philosophy third Series edited by H. D. LEWIS

Contemporary Indian Philosophy edited by RADHAKRISHNAN and J. H. MUIRHEAD 2nd edition

Contemporary Philosophy in Australia edited by ROBERT BROWN and C. D. ROLLINS

The Discipline of the Cave by J. N. FINDLAY

Doctrine and Argument in Indian Philosophy by NINIAN SMART

Essays in Analysis by ALICE AMBROSE

Ethics by NICOLAI HARTMANN translated by STANTON COIT 3 vols

The Foundations of Metaphysics in Science by ERROL E. HARRIS

Freedom and History by H. D. LEWIS

The Good Will: A Study in the Coherence Theory of Goodness by H. J. PATON

Hegel: A Re-examination by J. N. FINDLAY

Hegel's Science of Logic translated by W. H. JOHNSTON and L. G. STRUTHERS 2 vols.

History of Aesthetic by B. BOSANQUET 2nd edition

History of English Utilitarianism by E. ALBEE

History of Psychology by G. S. BRETT edited by R. S. PETERS abridged one volume edition 2nd edition

Human Knowledge by BERTRAND RUSSELL

A Hundred Years of British Philosophy by RUDOLF METZ translated by J. H. HARVEY, T. E. JESSOP, HENRY STURT

Ideas: A General Introduction to Pure Phenomenology by EDMUND HUSSERL translated by W. R. BOYCE GIBSON

Identity and Reality by EMILE MEYERSON

Imagination by E. J. FURLONG

Indian Philosophy by RADHAKRISHNAN 2 vols revised 2nd edition
Introduction to Mathematical Philosophy by BERTRAND RUSSELL 2nd edition
Kant's First Critique by H. W. CASSIRER
Kant's Metaphysic of Experience by J. H. PATON
Know Thyself by BERNADINO VARISCO translated by GUGLIELMO SALVADORI
Language and Reality by WILBUR MARSHALL URBAN
Lectures on Philosophy by G. E. MOORE
Lecturers on Philosophy by G. E. MOORE edited by C. LEWY
Matter and Memory by HENRI BERGSON translated by N. M. PAUL and W. S. PALMER
Memory by BRIAN SMITH
The Modern Predicament by H. J. PATON
Natural Rights by D. G. RITCHIE 3rd edition
Nature, Mind and Modern Science by E. HARRIS
The Nature of Thought by BRAND BLANSHARD
On Selfhood and Godhood by C. A. CAMPBELL
Our Experience of God by H. D. LEWIS
Perception by DON LOCKE
The Phenomenology of Mind by G. W. F. HEGEL translated by SIR JAMES BAILLIE revised 2nd edition
Philosophy in America by MAX BLACK
Philosophical Papers by G. E. MOORE
Philosophy and Illusion by MORRIS LAZEROWITZ
Philosophy and Political Economy by JAMES BONAR
Philosophy and Religion by AXEL HAGERSTROM
Philosophy of Space and Time by MICHAEL WHITEMAN
Philosophy of Whitehead by W. MAYS
The Platonic Tradition in Anglo-Saxon Philosophy by J. H. MUIRHEAD
The Principal Upanisads by RADHAKRISHNAN
The Problems of Perception by R. J. HIRST
Reason and Goodness by BLAND BLANSHARD
The Relevance of Whitehead by IVOR LECLERC
The Science of Logic by G. W. F. HEGEL
Some Main Problems of Philosophy by G. S. MOORE
Studies in the Metaphysics of Bradley by SUSHIL KUMAR SAXENA
The Theological Frontier of Ethics by W. G. MACLAGAN
Time and Free Will by HENRI BERGSON translated by F. G. POGSON
The Transcendence of the Cave by J. N. FINDLAY
Values and Intentions by J. N. FINDLAY
The Ways of Knowing: or the Methods of Philosophy by W. P. MONTAGUE

Muirhead Library of Philosophy

EDITED BY H. D. LEWIS

A LAYMAN'S QUEST

By the same author

ACTION

A LAYMAN'S QUEST

BY

SIR MALCOLM KNOX

LONDON · GEORGE ALLEN & UNWIN LTD
NEW YORK · HUMANITIES PRESS INC

FIRST PUBLISHED IN 1969

SBN 04 201014 4

PRINTED IN GREAT BRITAIN
in 11 *on* 12 *point Imprint type*
BY UNWIN BROTHERS LIMITED
WOKING AND LONDON

To

St Mary's College, St Andrews

CONTENTS

PREFACE

This book, like its predecessor, *Action*, is based on Gifford Lectures delivered in the University of Aberdeen. In dealing with moral philosophy in the first series of lectures, I was on my own ground. I had had a training in the subject under the best of teachers, R. G. Collingwood, and it was the topic of my professorial chair. In this book I trespass on the ground of theologians and historians: in their disciplines I am an amateur, but in Scotland there is no law of trespass and I hope to escape prosecution. Nevertheless, I am conscious of the temerity of my enterprise, and I may well be told that I have read the wrong books and failed to read the right ones. Still, perhaps my errors may encourage some ecclesiastical historian to demolish them, just as Lessing hoped for a refutation of Reimarus (a hope still largely unfulfilled). At the end of my second course of lectures in Aberdeen an eminent theologian paid me a great compliment: 'It was a good statement of a bad case.' In this book I have amplified the statement, but I cannot hope to have made the case any better.

My quest for what it is reasonable to believe began nearly fifty years ago. The answer has varied from time to time under the influence of friends and of books of varying kinds. In this book I have set forth in an historical order an account of the books which, at different times and in various ways, have most influenced my thinking. This is not the order in which I have studied them, and in these chapters I may not always have made plain what I have accepted from them and what I have rejected. I hope, however, that, at the end, my position may have become clear, and, in any case, inferences may be correctly drawn from my selection of passages to quote or to summarize. The method which I have adopted has inevitably involved some repetition, since the same point crops up again and again in the literature; but I have tried to keep repetition to a minimum.

My first chapter attempts to show that it is reasonable to have a religious belief. My final chapter indicates some of the theological and philosophical implications of the belief, which, after the historical survey in the intervening chapters, I have come to find reasonable.

Just as, in *Action*, I wrote rather for the general reader interested in moral problems than for professional philosophers, so here I have written primarily for other laymen who may share my interest in the New Testament and the beginnings of Christianity. Some of my summaries may be news to them. Although my conclusions are far from orthodoxy, I sometimes wonder if many devout Church members really believe more than I do.

To theologians I must admit, in the words of Kant in *Das Ende aller Dinge*, that *Ich bin mir . . . meines Unvermögens, hierin einen neuen und glücklichen Versuch zu machen, bewusst*. (To the laity: 'I am well aware of my inability to make a new and successful attempt at this subject.')

I am deeply indebted to two friends—Professor H. J. Paton, FBA, and Rev. Professor Matthew Black, FBA—who read my typescript. Their criticisms and suggestions have saved me from many errors and helped me to improve some of my arguments. They are not to be taken as agreeing with anything that I say, and all error, imperfection, and inadequacy in this book is to be laid to my charge alone.

I also acknowledge with gratitude the work done by my friends Miss J. S. M. Allan and Mrs A. H. M. Marshall, who between them typed the first draft in 1967.

An author's chief debt is usually to his wife. That my debt is owed to her in a special way for the time during which this book has been prepared for the press, my friends will understand.

T. M. KNOX

Crieff
October 1968

CHAPTER 1

FAITH

In *Action* I argued that the moral life is a rational life: that the development of moral experience runs *pari passu* with the development of reason, where 'reason' means not the mere intellect (Kant's *Verstand*) but the full development of self-consciousness, a synthesis of what are called 'intellect' and 'will', something more like Hegel's *Vernunft*. I argued further that the supreme development of the moral consciousness implies an absolute devotion which chimes in with religion. But, if so, then what the rationality of the moral consciousness requires is a religion which reason can accept. What religion is this? Is there, to use Kant's phrase, a 'religion within the bounds of reason alone' which can be accepted not only by reason but by the believer with his whole soul? If so, what is it? The question is hard, especially because certain developments in Christian theology, in the last century or so, may seem to give good grounds for the question asked by the Superior of the Novice in *Melmoth the Wanderer*: 'My deluded child, when had reason anything to do with religion?'[1] The question expects the answer 'never', but I still think it is worth asking whether, as chiming in with our experience of duty, there is not a religion that can be accepted by the reason which has developed up to the consciousness of duty, and, if so, what that religion is.

There are many today, however, who would regard this question as not worth asking at all. Religion has become for them an almost meaningless word. They neither worship nor pray, and apparently are quite content to live as if churches did not exist. If religion does not interest them, however, we may well ask what does. To all appearance the answer is: sport and gambling.

Something has gone wrong when the seriousness of human life, as distinct from animal life, is trivialized in this way. Religion is one essential feature in the life of mind, and it is not surprising if those who ignore it become disorientated and *déracinés*.

Since the time of the Romantics, modern Europe has often looked back to the Middle Ages with a nostaligia for that epoch when life was coherent because people knew where they were going and how to guide their lives. This unity of purpose and conviction made possible the great achievements of the time, Gothic

[1] London, 1820, i, p. 249.

cathedrals, the *Summae* of Thomas Aquinas, the works of Dante, achievements which we may envy, whatever their background of squalor and superstition. This was a civilization with theology as its kernel. Its products were products of faith, not only religious faith, but a belief that the fabric of civilization was worth not only preserving but weaving further.

What a contrast with the world of today! Our world is often compared, and rightly, with the dying years of the Roman Empire. We have lost faith in our civilization to such an extent that men need 'incentives' before they will work. Economic security is a watchword, but lip service does not produce the reality; the reality recedes because there are insufficient 'incentives' for co-operative effort. Our modern art witnesses to the 'failure of nerve' characteristic of a dying culture. What dominates in our architecture is great rectangular blocks of offices or flats, repeated with monotonous regularity, whatever the environment. Painting and music may be the expression of scepticism or bewilderment or anger, but hardly of any faith.

In a sceptical age dogmatisms flourish too, and we have plenty of them, whether Roman, or Barthian, or Marxist, or naturalistic. Their very multiplicity witnesses to the fact that there is no kernel left in our civilization; it is dying, if not dead.

And yet man needs a faith if he is not simply to descend to an animal level. During the six years war this nation was fused into a unity by the genius of Winston Churchill. If the 'spirit of Dunkirk' or the heroism that endured the bombing of cities is to be recaptured, then a new faith is needed to rouse the imagination of the people and to provide stimulus and principles for action. It will not be enough to repeat familiar dogmatisms; doubts about them are too deep-seated, and in any case they are too well-founded in scientific and historical criticism. We have to ask afresh the questions that most modern philosophy eschews: What is man? What sort of a world does he live in? What is his chief end?

The questions are old; the answers may be old too; but, if so, they need to be re-stated in a form which takes account of the processes which have led to their negation. The civilization which succeeded the Greco-Roman had Christian theology as its kernel. Science has claims to be regarded as the kernel of the seventeenth century and later. But its inadequacy is now patent. It cannot tell us how or to what end we should use the tools which it has put into our hands.

Once a civilization dies it cannot be revived. The gates of the future are open. The task before us today is to lay proper foundations for what lies beyond them, or, in other words, to formulate the faiths on which a new civilization can be built. This task is an ambitious one, but it is the task to which philosophers and theologians today are called.

To the first two of the questions to which I have just referred I offered answers in *Action*: (i) Man is not simply a member of a biological species; whatever his natural origin, he is capable of a moral and spiritual life and is not as he ought to be unless he actualizes that capacity. Hegel once put the point well when he said: 'Just because man *knows* that he is an animal, he ceases to be an animal and attains knowledge of himself as spirit.'[1] (ii) The world in which man lives is one capable of being known, one in which morality, as distinct from jungle law, is possible, and one in which beauty is discoverable. The natural world of fact has supranatural significance.

To the third question, What is man's chief end?, the Scottish Shorter Catechism (1648) provides an answer, namely 'to glorify God and enjoy him for ever'. No better may have been provided, but humanists and atheists will disagree. What, however, do they substitute? So far as I can see, either 'to be, and to make others, as happy as possible', or, 'to reduce suffering as far as possible'. The qualification 'as far as possible' is a recognition that to make happiness or the reduction of suffering a paramount aim in this life is to embark on an enterprise as hopeless as that of Sisyphus. Nevertheless, for those who think more of man's origin and his finitude than of his spiritual destiny, there may be no alternative.

To speak of 'spiritual destiny', however, is to reach at least the outskirts of religion, and to the problem of faith and reason it is now necessary to turn.

To associate reason with religion is not necessarily to expect to have a religion within the bounds of reason *alone*; on the contrary, there can be no religion without faith, or otherwise religion would collapse into philosophy or science. Faith, however, need not be a defiance of evidence, or simply irrational. It is lack of faith that can sometimes be unreasonable. For example, scientific inquiry would be unreasonable if it were not accompanied by faith in the possibility of success, by faith in the intelligibility of nature.

Man as mind or spirit is not satisfied by living on the animal

[1] *Werke*,[1] X, i, p. 104.

plane, by getting what the animals get; he craves beauty, goodness, and truth (however often this may be forgotten or unrealized today). These are abstract nouns and they have all the appearance of Professor Maclagan's 'values'.[1] But to avoid using them would involve too much circumlocution. The point is that in our imaginative, intellectual, and moral life we find ourselves, once we are conscious of our transcendence of nature, under compulsion. The artist, the scientist, the moral agent, finds that he must act in certain ways if he is not to be false to his calling or his higher self. And it is convenient to describe this compulsion on action by calling it a quest for beauty, truth, and goodness. This quest does not invariably succeed; but sometimes it does, and this is man's discovery of the real world, not the natural order but the spiritual order.

Man's quest for beauty, truth, and goodness is not the chasing of a will-o'-the-wisp but a response to objectivity, and so, as I have said, a quest which sometimes is successful. This will be denied. Beauty, it will be said, is only in the eye of the beholder, goodness merely characterizes actions which we approve or which happen to please us or which are socially useful, truth is just what happens to work and so to subserve our subjective needs. For example, the view from the Knock of Crieff is in my eyes one of great magnificence and beauty; but in the eighteenth century it would have usually been regarded as grim, barbarous, and ugly. Thus beauty is only a matter of personal taste. This is superficial. It does not explain, for example, the continued existence of artistic criticism. What a man finds beautiful will depend on his upbringing and education; toil is the price at which the gods sell their blessings to men. To say that 'this is beautiful' just means 'I like it' ignores the seriousness with which beauty has been sought, the uplift, inspiration, and refreshment which are experienced when it is found. 'It takes us out of ourselves' as we say. Nothing could be less subjective. It also fails to explain why masterpieces are recognized as such, century after century, by those with the knowledge to appreciate them. Ask an artist or a scientist why he works as he does at his picture or his problem in the laboratory. The answer will seldom be 'because it amuses me', for that would put the work on the level of a hobby. The artist must get his picture exactly right; the scientist must find the inescapable answer to his problem. The claim of beauty and of truth is as abso-

[1] *Vide Action*, pp. 226–7.

lute as that of goodness. Subjectivist views of truth have seldom presented any appeal to scientists or historians or philosophers.

What is being argued is not that beauty, goodness, and truth are simply there to be apprehended by a sort of sense-perception. On the contrary, their discovery is the end of a sort of spiritual quest; the subject and the object coalesce. The quest is a response to reality, possible only because the heart of reality is also the heart of man's spirit.

It may be said that to find beauty, goodness, and truth in the world is to take too optimistic a view. Nature is red in tooth and claw. Villains are commoner than saints. If truth can be found, error is commoner. A candid view of the world would see in it a riot of ugliness, evil, and falsehood. This may be true. But it is saner to give full force to the experience of beauty, heroism, truth, for these occur. In the vast universe man appears, a tiny spot, insignificant, if size or vastness be our criterion. And yet it is *for* the mind and spirit of man that all this vastness exists. Not by the earth do we judge, or by what fertilizes it, or by the root or the stem or the leaf of the rose, but by the flower. The universe has in it the possibility of glory, a possibility made actual by man when he rises to the heights of his potential spirituality, and, in the energy of his spirit, actualizes the latent potentialities of the object and so enjoys beauty, goodness, and truth.

These make absolute claims upon him only because, as spirit, he is capable of recognizing them and accepting them. And, in doing so, he finds at last, if he has asked the question, an understanding of this experience as a justification for a belief in God. Whether an argument on these lines could ever bring to a faith in God anyone brought up without any such faith, I do not know. It might perplex him if he tried to explain, if he felt them, the absolute claims of duty or truth. But these claims seem to me to become intelligible to a believer in God, and to give to such a believer who seeks reasons for his belief a harmony between the religion he was taught in youth and the scientific, or artistic, or philosophical, or moral experience which he has had as an adult. What better explanation is there?

Beauty, goodness, and truth are all forms of perfection, and it is worth asking how we come by this notion. No type of empiricism can provide a satisfactory answer.[1] For example, it is suggested

[1] Professor J. N. Wright has pointed out to me that I may have learnt this line of argument first from the *Third Meditation* of Descartes.

that we see that x is a better man than y, and y than z, and then by extrapolation reach the notion of perfection—*id quo melius cogitari nequit* (that than which nothing better can be thought). But this cannot be accepted. If I find that x is taller than y and y than z, I do not produce by extrapolation the notion of perfect height. I assess the relative heights of the three men by using a standard, a foot rule or the like. But the comparison in terms of moral goodness already implies the standard of goodness itself, i.e. the standard of perfection. We cannot describe two things as unequal unless we first know what equality is; and equality—a perfection—we have never encountered. If it is then suggested that we do just encounter perfection, e.g. in the 'Mona Lisa', or the 'St Matthew Passion', and thus derive the concept of perfection from experience, the suggestion must be met with a denial. Nothing in this world is perfect, for everything is finite and therefore limited. The 'Mona Lisa' and the 'St Matthew Passion' may be beautiful but they are not beauty.

The craving for beauty, truth, and goodness is at once a response to reality and a discovery of it. It is also an activity of man as spirit, not nature. Consciousness of man as spirit is a consciousness of a clash between what I am and what I potentially am, a clash within the self between finite and infinite. This is where the transition to religious faith occurs. The spirit of man is the candle of the Lord. The quest for the ideal is not motivated by Platonic forms or by 'values', for these cannot impose obligations on us. Devotion to these ideals is like the worship of God whose nature they partially express, and is intelligible only as the response of self-transcendence to the spiritual reality present in man implicitly from the start. 'Thou hast made us for thyself and our hearts are restless until they find rest in thee.' Countless thousands who have climbed the heights of moral experience could never have reached them, let alone dwelt on them, without faith in that divine power of goodness, both outside and inside themselves, which is part of what we mean by God.[1]

The artist's devotion to his art, the scientist's to truth, are just as categorical as the call of duty. Kant speaks of *reverence* for the moral law, and it is equally in place to speak of reverence for beauty and truth. But these abstractions cannot be worshipped, and worship has been characteristic of mankind, except when humility

[1] This sentence is an adaptation of one by Sir Arthur Bryant in *Illustrated London News*, January 29, 1955.

has been at a discount. Devotion to beauty, truth, and goodness is intelligible as the worship of God and the development of the spiritual life.

This argument will not appeal to humanists. They believe that 'this world is all we have and all we need; that we should try to lead full and happy lives ourselves and, as part of them, help to make it easier for other people to do the same'.[1] This can be interpreted in two ways: on the one hand, it may be regarded as a programme for a community of animals; on the other hand, 'this world' may mean the world of the spiritual life, and a full life will be one in which religion and the worship of God play a part. It is the former interpretation which seems to accord with most humanist writing. It forgets or has not yet learnt that man cannot be happy without devotion to spiritual ends.

This is the plight of many adolescents today. Not only have they no religion, they have no art either, but make a cult of ugliness. To encounter some of them in groups is to be reminded of savages. Taught to be human, all too human, they live for the pleasure of the hour. So they are not happy but only noisy, and, underneath, bewildered, disorientated. If man is to live a human and not an animal life, he cannot live on bread alone. This means that in one sense the happy life which the humanist desiderates is impossible, as I have argued above. He that increaseth knowledge increaseth sorrow. Human life is a serious business, and, to anyone who reflects, it is a tragedy which only religion can overcome. Henley's 'unconquerable soul' is bluster. Shelley knew better, or at least did not shrink from the truth:

> He has outsoared the shadow of our night;
> Envy and calumny, and hate and pain,
> And that unrest which men miscall delight,
> Can touch him not, and torture not again.

It is for reflection that the tragic aspect of life exists, and yet it is reflection too which perseveres towards beauty, goodness, and truth, and finds in that pursuit the happiness which outsoars the evils that Shelley lists. This perserverance would be unintelligible if the mind or spirit of man did not find itself in the world; it is as if the world were on the side of these ideals. It is this

[1] H. J. Blackham, Chairman of the British Humanist Association, in a Sunday newspaper, November 1966. I have lost the precise reference.

mystery for which religious faith alone can supply a reasonable explanation.

Humanism, it is often said, is parasitic on the religion which it rejects. If suffering is to be alleviated simply because it is suffering, then there is no difference in principle between exempting a wrongdoer from punishment and releasing into the open air a bird trapped and frightened indoors. Equality as an ideal is senseless unless it is given a religious foundation, namely that inequalities are insignificant in comparison with the equidistance of all men from God.[1] Humanitarian zeal, not based on respect for man as spirit, readily becomes dictatorial; what begins as nineteenth-century liberalism sinks into its opposite, belief in regimentation by the State. By abandoning the religion which made its ideals intelligible, humanism has cut the ground from below its own feet. To concentrate on the purely human is to take the route which leads to the beehive and the anthill. This is something which the humanist may regret. Sometimes he may see that he has had too lofty a view of human *nature* by believing that men were naturally good and that all that was necessary was to remove hindrances in the way of their happiness. But if this leads to a rigidly planned economy, the humanist can feel no *remorse*, because that implies a sense of sin, an alienation from a central source of goodness and truth.[2] No doubt a psychologist is then produced who will explain remorse away as the fruit of delusions, and the mind of the victim will then be swept and garnished, ready for the reception of worse devils.

Humanists will not deny the progress that physical science has made in the last three or four centuries, but they seem to ignore the advance of the religious consciousness in the same period. Heretics are no longer burnt at the stake, nor are witches drowned; slavery has been abolished. Are Christians today not entitled to hold that these changes represent a deepening of the religious consciousness, a deeper insight into what Jesus taught men about God?

Professor A. G. N. Flew will not mind being numbered with the humanists, and his well-known views merit attention at this point. He tells us that 'a thorough and systematic apologetic must start from the beginning, and hence must be capable of displaying . . . what it is proposed that the term *God* should mean, how its sup-

[1] This is drawn from E. Voegelin: *Plato* (Baton Rouge, 1966), p. 234.
[2] *Vide* L. Hyde: *The Prospects of Humanism* (London, 1931), p. 195.

posed object could be identified as a subject of conversation, and what job . . . its sponsors want to introduce the word to do'. Professor Flew is sure that this is an impossible enterprise; the concept of God, he says, is 'botched up' and for it 'no legitimate or explanatory work' can be found.[1]

In thus talking about the 'concept' of God, Professor Flew may be sinning in good company, for Kant apparently put the concept of God on a level with the concept of a hundred dollars. But in discussing the 'word' God, Professor Flew is as far from understanding religion as the man was from understanding a string quartet when he described it as the noise made by scraping horses' tails on catgut.

It is God and not the word 'God' or the 'concept' of God with which religion is concerned, and if Professor Flew had penetrated so far within the religious consciousness, his criticisms might have been more relevant. In reply to him, we could tell him, for example, that God is worshipped. Men have worshipped all sorts of things and this is why their conception (not concept) of God has altered. The *word* 'God', which interests Professor Flew, means at least the object of worship. The lexicographical question, however, is easier to answer than such a question as: How can God be infinite and yet the object of man's worship? Here no help can be expected from Professor Flew, because the question can be answered, if at all, only from within religious experience and not from outside.

Asked about the 'concept' of God, the religious man will ignore the word 'concept' and may say that God is spirit and that they who worship him must worship him in spirit and in truth. If Professor Flew pulls this to pieces, as doubtless he can, it is because he has so revolted against his religious upbringing as to forget that the language of religion is inescapably metaphorical, or as to be no longer able to glimpse the truth behind the metaphor.

There is a further point. Man craves forgiveness for his misdeeds. To offend a friend, or to fail him, disrupts the relationship, and it produces an agony which persists until the friendship is restored by forgiveness. If I am right in associating the absoluteness of moral claims with religion, then moral failure separates the sinner from God; if he repents, he has been taught to seek forgiveness, and he believes that a contrite heart will not be despised. If this sounds too like '*Dieu me pardonnera, c'est son métier*',

[1] *Mind*, 1967, p. 295.

it at least provides an intelligible answer to Professor Flew's enquiry as to the 'job' which the sponsors of the word 'God' want the word to do.

I have suggested that our experience of beauty, truth, and goodness is a reasonable ground for making the *venture of faith* in a God whose nature is, or is expressed through, these characteristics. Professor Flew says that 'no philosopher needs to be ashamed of wanting his beliefs to be true and *to be known to be true*'.[1] This is to ask for the impossible. A belief known to be true is no longer a belief, but knowledge. 'Believing where we cannot prove' is a more sensible statement than Professor Flew's.

Aristotle, starting from thinking, came, in that great passage from the *Metaphysics* with which Hegel ended his system of philosophy, to the existence of God: 'Thought thinks itself by participation in the object of thought; for it becomes an object of thought in coming into contact with and thinking its objects, so that thought and the object of thought are the same. . . . The actuality of thought is life, and God is that actuality. . . . God is a living being, eternal and best . . . for this *is* God.' This is the argument from finite to infinite: *thinking* in man is the spark of the divine. But how is this to be understood if God, the infinite, is not also regarded as creator, the creator who has made man in his image, that is to say, possessed of spiritual potentiality? It is true that faith in God as creator invites such questions as: Who made God? What was he doing before he created the world? To the second of these questions one of the Fathers replied: He was making a Hell to contain those who ask silly questions. Reason can never take us all the way. To the question: Why anything? there is no answer. It is reasonable to try to explain or make sense of our experience, but unreasonable to ask why there is any experience or reality at all. The point comes when we have to end with Sir Thomas Browne who loved to pursue his 'reason to an *O Altitudo*!'.[2] But this is not the end of reason; it is only the end of argument; and it is reasonable to see that argument must have an end.[3]

Those who will not make this venture of faith may perhaps have reflected too litle on the hold that religion has had on mankind. No doubt religion has been responsible for great evils, and some

[1] *God and Philosophy* (London, 1966), p. 181. My italics.

[2] *Religio Medici*, § 9.

[3] This coheres with Professor Flew's remarks on explanation (*God and Philosophy* (edn cit., pp. 82–3). But he stops short of *O Altitudo*!

religions are worse than others and no better than superstition. To maintain, however, that all religion is an illusion with no future is to condemn the man in the street (who is neither scientist nor philosopher) to be caught in the clutches of either superstition or total scepticism. Both of these are irrational. If beliefs and theories are rejected because they are false, then some knowledge of truth is implied: if because they are unconvincing, then knowledge of what would convince is implied. In both cases complete scepticism is a self-contradiction.

The strongest argument against associating reason with religion may be the continued existence (and perhaps success) of the Roman Catholic Church, despite its promulgation, during the last century or so, of doctrines *de fide* which are indefensible by reason unaided. In 1870 Lord Clarendon wrote, referring to Papal infallibility: 'This monstrous assault on the reason of mankind is the only chance of mankind being roused to resistance against being insolently thrust back into the darkest periods of Church despotism.'[1] This affront to the reason of mankind, however, would seem to have strengthened the Roman Church rather than have weakened it. And in any case that Church has never disparaged reason, as Luther and Barth, for example, have done.

It may be said that so far from man being made in the image of God, man has made God in *his* image, and this is the irrationality of anthropomorphism. It is true that when man comes to try to describe the God in whom he believes through his experience of absolutes which call for his reverence, he must use the only vocabulary he has. Man's spiritual life at its highest is always conscious of its finitude and a beyond. But the beyond cannot be less than the highest reach of man's spiritual endeavour. Therefore man must ascribe to God the perfection of such spiritual achievements as he may have attained, and in addition he must ascribe personality to God, even if this be only an attempt by metaphor to ascribe to God at least the highest category that man ascribes to himself.

In a television programme (January 12, 1967) pupils in a secondary school voiced their views in the class hour devoted to religious instruction. A girl said quite bluntly: 'Man invented God, and the need for this invention has gone.' A boy added: 'We have to have this hour of instruction. We are told this and that about God. But there is no argument. God is man's invention.' Perhaps they had a

[1] N. Blakiston: *The Roman Question* (London, 1962), pp. 398–9.

perplexed and bewildered teacher. If man invented God, and the invention seems to have been very widespread in cultures that had little or no connection with one another, it is reasonable to ask why man invented him. I do not know how these children would have answered the question. If man lived on a natural plane alone, he could hardly raise questions about the source or meaning or destiny of his life. If he invented God, it was because he had raised these questions, and so had risen above the natural, happy, idle life of the animals to an intellectual level; and once there is an elevation to that level, there is the possibility of reflecting on it and so of elevation to the level of spirit. This is the self-transcendence to which I have alluded so often (in *Action*). To reflect on an achievement is already to have gone beyond it, transcended it.

Great ingenuity and massive learning are required in order to prove the impossible. The curious thing is that they are not lacking, whether it is a matter of extracting the date of the end of the world from Daniel and Revelation, or proving that God is a human invention. I quote only one example of the latter from a book published in 1953 on the *Origins of Christianity* by Mr A. Robertson, who appears to be a Marxist. There is no doubt about his learning. His first chapter is headed: How man made God. Even if this question were satisfactorily answered, it would prove nothing about religion today. The argument from origins is always hazardous. Development proceeds by negating the starting-point. Mr Robertson begins with magicians and rulers, and then argues that it was from them that man constructed the idea of God. How and why? The leap from finite to infinite is unexplained. It is also unintelligible, unless man as thinker had the idea of the infinite implicit in his very thinking itself. No doubt the idea of God has changed. Men have worshipped strange gods. The Christian idea is not that of the Jews, though it was first learnt from them. Even the Christian idea varies. A book entitled *Honest to God*, reviving some ideas expounded sixty years ago by Rev. Dr R. J. Campbell, has made a sensation and become a best-seller. The real point is that, so far from inventing anything, man has been conscious in diverse ways, in beauty, goodness, and truth, of something transcending himself and his world, something which, when he is humble enough, he must worship.

Reverence or worship has been a human characteristic for long past, and men have worshipped very odd things. But to say that man invented God is to repudiate worship and reverence altogether. It is to deny all absolute claims, whether of beauty, goodness, or truth, and to sink to an animal level, a level of lower animals, for even dogs seem to have an inkling sometimes of what worship is. If God is thought to be an old gentleman living in the sky, then indeed the girl was right to say that this was an invention or a myth. But if she had been asked whether she reverenced or worshipped anything, her answer might have brought her nearer religion and started the argument which the boy desired. But the argument might be about the nature of God, rather than about his existence. Of the existence there is no proof; we cannot get beyond belief. But the belief is reasonable for those who are conscious of the spiritual realm to which man belongs and in which he sometimes lives, and who therefore are worshippers of what in that realm is supreme and perfect.

In his lecture on *Kant's Moral Theology* (British Academy, 1963) Professor W. H. Walsh argues that Kant's endeavour to make the moral consciousness point beyond itself is 'finally and irretrievably shattered. Social scientists show that the feeling of moral obligation is part of an attitude which is socially fostered and serves a vital social purpose. Kant looked on the moral law as an object of awe; social scientists strip it of its mystery by explaining its function in the social whole.' For more than one reason this seems to me to be very superficial. First, it takes us back to utilitarian ethics, about which I wrote more than enough in my book on *Action*. Secondly, of course, morality is socially useful, but it does not follow at all that its utility is our reason for trying to abide by it, unless we are utilitarians. A belief may be very useful, but, if we believe it, we believe it because we think it is true, unless we are pragmatists. Thirdly, even if the methods of the social sciences differ from those used in the physical science, they still must have their limitations if their use of the word 'science' is to be taken seriously. In so far as they do not rest on observation alone, they are employed by those who inevitably bring with them to the subject-matter their own presuppositions, and then inevitably find what they are looking for. A true account of social life would interpret the mundane by reference to the highest achievements of the spirit of man. But the tendency of social science is to take things as they are, to deal with facts, and not to consider what they could be in process of becoming; to concentrate on what are supposed to be facts (though they are often but answers to questionnaires), and to ignore the spirit which eludes scientific observation and cannot be confined within scientific categories. The point is made by Hegel, though in a different connection, when he is considering the supposed conflict between science and religion: 'Science takes things as they are; its understanding of them is based on empirical grounds; it seeks for causes and effects, but those that it finds are finite too. Knowledge of this kind never leaves and never wants to leave the sphere of the finite. Thus it does not need God; it lies outside religion and has nothing to do with it. Religion is concerned with the infinite, and with the finite only in so far as that shines in the light of the infinite.'[1] Lastly, as I have urged, reverence is not only for the moral law, but for beauty and truth also. Reverence for these may be explained away too, but, whatever may be said about beauty, the social scientist who explained away our reverence for truth would be betraying his claim to be a scientist.

Insensitivity to art is possible, but those who suffer from it are deprived of one essential element in the intellectual or spiritual life of man. Lack of religious experience is a similar deprivation. The worship of God needs faith, but it is an experience which the worshipper today finds correspondent with that of generations before him.

The experience has not always been the same. Man's conception of God has changed. If there are passages in the Psalms and the Prophets whch speak to us today with an authentic voice, there are others which we can only repudiate. God is not like that.

Many will urge that this eclecticism is impermissible when the New Testament is under consideration, but this contention is unreasonable. There are too many contradictions there.

It is reasonable to grant all that is said about the evil done in the name of God and religion, and yet, while forsaking many orthodox doctrines, to refuse to abandon religion altogether, and to continue to worship in spirit and in truth. It may be unreasonable to do otherwise.

The faith for which I have argued in this chapter does not go beyond deism or natural religion. God as love and heavenly father is something taught by Jesus, something which reason *may* accept, but which by itself it cannot propound or prove.

I have argued that truth, goodness, and beauty seem to make absolute claims on us, and that our experience of these claims makes reasonable a faith in God. It might be said that we have

[1] Paraphrased from *Phil. d. Rel.*, ed. Lasson, Leipzig, 1930, i, pp. 20–1.

experience too of love and fatherliness, and that this might be a rational ground for believing in God as a loving heavenly father. But duty is an absolute demand on all of us (unless we are utilitarians), and truth and beauty make absolute demands on scientists and artists. It does not seem to me that love and fatherliness make demands of the same kind. Experience of them makes it reasonable to *accept* a conception of God as heavenly father, but does not afford a ground for propounding or proving it.

The Christian religion is the religion of our civilization, the one in which we have been brought up, and the question is: What in it is it reasonable to believe? Alone of the great religions, Christianity appeals to historical events as its basis. The Apostles' Creed anchors the faith to history. To question the truth of the New Testament is therefore to question the truth of Christianity. The question was raised in an acute form in the eighteenth century; it has been treated in a variety of ways since then; sometimes it has been side-tracked; but the question: What think ye of Christ?, where the operative word is 'think', challenges us today with undiminished force.

Scientific attacks on the credibility of miracles seem to me to be less serious for the Christian than the historical probing to which I have referred. The world of which science gives an account is not the real world of our experience, but an abstraction. Neither beauty nor the 'unremembered acts of kindness and of love' are within the scope of scientific instruments; and it is an error to dismiss *a priori* the possibility of miracle.[1] No doubt the Church has made unwise claims in the past about matters within the competence of science; but it need not make such claims; its concern is not with nature, the domain of science, butwith the supra-natural. Hence, it need not clash with science at all, even if science clashes with it. Historical claims, however, the Church must make, and therefore it stands at the bar of history and cannot evade historical investigation. A denial of this assertion will come before us in due course.

Jane Austen once described herself as a 'partial, prejudiced, and ignorant historian', and as an amateur in this field I merit a similar description. However, I am not attempting to write a history of New Testament criticism and interpretation during the last two centuries; for the century from 1861 this has been admirably

[1] On miracle, see below, Ch. 7.

done by Bishop Stephen Neill.[1] What I am attempting is a review, over the last two centuries, of some important ways which I regard as crucial, in which the historical problem has been raised and answered, and some endeavours to evade it, and I shall close by giving some indication of how the matter seems to me to stand today. This will provide my answer to the question what religious belief, within the bounds of reason, is compatible with my account of morality, or in general, my answer to the question: What is it reasonable to believe?

[1] *The Interpretation of the New Testament 1861–1961*. I have used the paperback, corrected edition, Oxford, 1966.

CHAPTER 2

REIMARUS

Albert Schweitzer begins his history of the Quest of the Historical Jesus with H. S. Reimarus, and we must begin there too. Reimarus, born in 1694, was a Professor of Oriental Languages at the Grammar School in Hamburg for forty years until his death in 1768. A book which he published in 1754 about the principal truths of natural religion received high commendation from Kant.[1]

In about 1744 he began work on an *Apology or Vindication for the Rational Worshippers of God*, and he continued to revise and enlarge his manuscript until 1767.

Of this work three manuscripts survive; none of them has been published in its entirety:

(i) In 1814 Reimarus's son presented to the University Library in Hamburg a manuscript which he said was throughout in his father's handwriting and represented the finally revised version of his work. It appears to be dated 1767.

(ii) A second manuscript copied from (i) by two amenuenses was bequeathed by Reimarus's son to the University Library of Göttingen. He said that he could not vouch for the accuracy of this copy.

(iii) A third manuscript is now in the possession of the Public Archives in Hamburg.

Between 1774 and 1778, in his *Beiträge zur Geschichte und Literatur*, Lessing published six extracts from Reimarus, saying that he had found the manuscript in the Wolfenbüttel Library, of which he was librarian. No author's name was given. Lessing called him 'my anonymous'. Only the first two of the extracts correspond with the text of manuscript (i). Lessing must have been using an earlier version, probably dated from about 1748. After the storm created by the sixth extract (*The Aim of Jesus and his Disciples*, with an excursus on the Resurrection), he complied with an order to send the manuscript to his employer, the Duke of Brunswick. What happened to it is unknown, but either it was returned to Lessing or else he retained in his own hands most of

[1] *Vide* the General Remark on Teleology at the end of the *Critique of Judgment*.

what Reimarus wrote about the Old Testament, since it was from him that C. A. E. Schmidt, *alias* Andreas Riem, received the material which he published in 1787 as *Further Unpublished Works of the Wolfenbüttel Fragmentist*, and this material was exclusively about the Old Testament.

Three further extracts were published in 1850–52 by Wilhelm Klose in the *Zeitschrift für historische Theologie*. These were taken from manuscript (iii).

In 1862 D. F. Strauss published a book on Reimarus in which he included further unpublished material after examining manuscript (iii) and one of the others. (From the second edition of his book, 1872, it appears that the other was (i).) Strauss sought to interpret Reimarus to the nineteenth century. He had thought of publishing him entire, but concluded that he belonged so clearly to the eighteenth century that he would have few readers in the nineteenth.[1]

In spite of what Strauss says, it seems to me to be a misfortune that so much of Reimarus remains unpublished. Schweitzer's encomium on him is well known, but it does not seem to have rescued him from neglect. The only English translation, and that of only a small part of *The Aim of Jesus and his Disciples*, was issued in 1879. A short summary of the extracts published by Lessing is contained in Dr Henry Chadwick's introduction to his edition of *Lessing's Theological Writings* (London, 1956).

The general nature of his work is thus described by Reimarus himself: 'The propositions contained herein are not in the nature of a catechism; they remain within the limits of a reasonable worship of God and the practice of philanthropy and virtue. I wished fully to satisfy myself and my rising doubts. I could not but thoroughly investigate the faith that had raised so many difficulties for me, in order to discover whether it could subsist with the rules of truth or not.'[2]

[1] This account of the Reimarus manuscripts and their partial publication I have derived from (i) D. F. Strauss: *H. S. Reimarus* (Leipzig, 1872. I have not seen the earlier edition). (ii) Lessing's *Werke* (Berlin, 1956) vii. p. 872. (iii) G. Pons: *G. E. Lessing et le Christianisme* (Paris, 1964), pp. 272–92. Unfortunately these three are all in disagreement on a number of points. In the main I I have followed Pons, since he is the most recent of those known to me who has studied the question. He provides a bibliography and states (p. 469) that the University Library of Hamburg expects to publish manuscript (i) *incessament*. The Librarian has kindly informed me that publication was expected early in 1969 by the Insel-Verlag, Frankfurt.

[2] Quoted in Lessing: *Anti-Goeze* 7, *Werke* (edn cit.) viii, p. 252.

He also said (apparently in the final manuscript) that his book had been written many years earlier, but in re-reading it he had enlarged some passages and shortened or altered others. He did not want to bring readers into error or to disturb people. His book was to lie concealed except from intelligent friends. He could not consent to its being printed until the age was more enlightened.[1]

Since I regard Reimarus's work as important, I proceed to give some account of it by summarizing the extracts published by Lessing, and supplementing them with material drawn from Strauss's book.

(i) The first of Lessing's extracts, *On the Toleration of the Deists*, attracted little notice. 'In so far as the pure doctrine of Christ as issued from his own mouth does not belong specifically to Judaism, but can become universal, it contains nothing but a rational practical religion. Consequently any reasonable man can conscientiously call himself a Christian. In both the Old Testament and the New there are non-Hebrew believers in a rational religion ('proselytes of the gate' in the Old, and those who 'feared God' in the New). They are accepted and allowed to participate in worship. But in the modern world rationalists are condemned and excluded even from civil rights, though sects of all fantastic kinds are tolerated somewhere or other. If men are supposed to believe without reason, what follows? It is because men are rational that they are above the animals and so have religion at all. The alternative to rational religion is superstition. The pure doctrine of Christ was corrupted by the Disciples when they imported into it Jewish beliefs about a Messiah and an inspired scripture.'

With some of this it is impossible not to sympathize, as my preceding chapter will have made clear. But the final sentence cannot be accepted. What is described as 'importation' was there already. The doctrine of Christ grew from the stock of Judaism. The assertion that what Jesus taught was a rational practical religion, valid for all men, assumes great importance, as we shall see, in the work of Kant and Hegel.

(ii) *Denunciation of Reason from the Pulpit*. This repeats some of the argument in the preceding essay. Some divines denounce reason on the ground that it was corrupted by Adam's fall. This is nonsense. Adam and Eve fell because they did not use their reason, and therefore the Fall cannot have corrupted it. The sects

[1] Lessing, vii, p. 871.

use reason in their arguments both to justify their own position and to attack others. Why, then, can they complain if reason is used against the fundamentals on which they agree? How can the fundamentals be justified otherwise than by reason?

This is fair enough. Attacks on reason destroy themselves, because, if they are not themselves based on reason, they are mere words without meaning.

(iii) *Impossibility of a Revelation which all Men can believe on Rational Grounds.* 'A divine revelation to *all* men at *all* times is a silly notion, unworthy of God's wisdom, because it would involve a perpetual succession of miracles and so a disruption of the natural order which God had created, and this would mean that God was contradicting himself. If, instead, a belief is advanced in a special revelation, then those to whom it is made become witnesses transmitting it to others; and they may be unreliable, and, like some Jewish prophets, carry no conviction.

'A revelation to the Jews is incredible. No one knew anything about them before Alexander the Great's time. Paul says he preaches to the ends of the earth, but there must have been a lot of pages missing from his atlas.[1]

'In 1744 only a very small proportion of mankind had ever heard of Christianity, let alone accepted it as a revelation. The trouble and expense of Missions is all lost: today there is no means of spreading Christianity among the "heathen". They have religions of their own. The eternal salvation or damnation of man cannot have depended on any special revelation; to suppose otherwise is to attribute to God monstrous injustice. Languages differ; the only possible revelation would be in the universal language of reason and conscience, the only language in which God can reveal himself at all.

'Since from the beginning of Christianity there were no translations of the New Testament, since copies were rare and dear, since the education of the young was bad, and since the laity were not allowed to read the Bible, then up to the present day scarcely one in a thousand Christians ever saw the Bible; and, amongst those who did, scarcely any had the skill to aid himself by exegesis in the difficult passages on which the articles of faith rest. From the beginning of Christianity, in the ages of darkness and ignorance, and even now in the Papal dominions, and even amongst most Protestants, there is simply a mere bigoted or catechismal faith. . . .

[1] This is unfair. Paul's atlas ended at the Pillars of Hercules.

They are just like parrots, taught by priests, most of whom are not competent to interpret the Scriptures.

'A book which is neither systematic nor clear, but is so written that a hundred different systems of theology can be derived from it, cannot be the vehicle of a divine revelation. . . . Moreover, a book cannot be a divine revelation if it contains a single untruth contradicting clear experience, history, sound reasoning, undeniable principles, or the rules of sound morality. The Pentateuch provides numerous examples of such untruths.

'Fortune and chance cannot be the ground of salvation or of a universal religion. It is a matter of chance what blind (statutory) faith we receive from our elders; Turks and Jews and the heathen receive their faith in this way; and it is just chance that we are born in a Christian society. If instead we seek a faith derived from biblical criticism, then few people have the necessary knowledge of history, languages, etc., and therefore a biblical revelation cannot be universal.

'We have no revelation of what and how many books contain the alleged revelation. There is nothing in the New Testament to justify the view that the two Testaments are canonical and that other books are apocryphal. A special revelation is out of the question.'

This is a long essay and the proliferation of arguments may become tedious. But it seems to be conclusive against an attempt to derive a special revelation from an infallible Bible. Reimarus does not discuss the idea of a special revelation to an infallible Church.

(iv) *The Passage of the Israelites through the Red Sea.* 'Even if the division of the Red Sea were accepted, with walls of water on either side, the story that the passage was effected in a single night is altogether incredible. There were said to be 600,000 men, besides women, children, flocks, and herds.' Reimarus calculates in detail that the whole calvalcade would be 187 miles long and would take several days to pass. 'The narrative in Exodus gives the impression that the floor of the Red Sea was flat and sandy, but it is nothing of the kind. It is rocky and probably impassable for vehicles.'

Although Lessing did not think so, Reimarus makes his case in this learned and witty essay. It must be added, however, that modern critics regard it as a naïve assumption to take the narrative as history instead of as a credal narrative based on tradition.

It is convenient to insert at this point some further fragments reported by Strauss. For example, the Pentateuch narratives are full of impossibilities and contradictions. All the cattle of the Egyptians are destroyed three or four times during a single spring. The number of Jews in Egyptian captivity is supposed to have risen from seventy (Genesis xlvi. 27) to three million in four generations (Numbers i reports 603,550 men at arms, so that the total number would be about three million). When the Israelites demanded flesh in the wilderness and quails were supplied, the ration was apparently 288 quails per person per day. The Pentateuch cannot be regarded as a revelation of God, for consider how much in it is a story of deceit and immorality. Abraham marries his half-sister, and this is characterized as an abomination in Leviticus. He offers his wife to Pharoah, pretending that she is his sister, and the same duplicity occurs with Isaac and Abimelech. And how could a God in whom we could believe tempt a man by telling him to slay his son?

Reimarus takes his conception of God from Jesus as, in his view, the teacher of a pure rational religion, but he rejects such things as the possibility of eternal punishment. The immoralities to which he draws attention are incontestable, and he may have reason on his side when he refuses to explain them away allegorically. The truth is that the conception of God has altered, but this has not been seen by the believers in an infallible Bible, and this includes believers in the England of the nineteenth century, Evangelicals and Tractarians alike, to mention none nearer our own day.

Mendelssohn and Eichhorn argued[1] against Reimarus that he transferred his moral ideas, leant from Christianity, to Genesis, instead of judging the Patriarchs by the standard of their own time. This is all very well, but it is not open to believers in an infallible Bible. Reimarus is certainly in the right against Newman, for example. Lessing said that Reimarus would have judged characters in Herodotus differently, and would have placed them in the context of their age. This may be so, but Herodotus has not been regarded as a divine revlation, and the Old Testament has.

(v) *The Books of the Old Testament were not written to Reveal a Religion.* 'The Old Testament knows nothing of the immortality of the soul or of Heaven and Hell. It is concerned with earthly

[1] *Vide* Strauss, *op. cit.*, pp. 83–4.

rewards for well-doing. Until the Babylonish captivity, what the Prophets did was to try to get the Israelites to worship the one God and keep the ordinances of Leviticus, but they did not have much success.

'The Psalms, Job, and Ecclesiastes clearly regard death as the end. Breath goes forth from the body and is just lost on the wind. Words like Heaven, Hell, spirit, appear in the Old Testament, but we must not read New Testament meanings into them.

'After the captivity, the Jews did begin to keep the law, even fanatically, and they also began to have a conception of the soul and its future fate. But this must have been due to the intellectual life of Babylon, and Jewish contact with the faith of other peoples. The Chaldaeans and the Egyptians, for example, had a doctrine of immortality. In the New Testament the Sadducees do not believe in the resurrection of the dead, but they are not pursued as heretics. On the contrary, they sit in the Sanhedrin, and this must have been because Jewish orthodoxy meant adhering to Moses and the Prophets, and not holding the new faith derived from non-Jewish sources.'

In this essay Reimarus is assuming that natural religion, or rational religion, included the doctrine of the immortality of the soul. Books of the Old Testament which know nothing of this doctrine therefore cannot possibly be regarded as revealing a religion which reason could accept. Reimarus seems to forget that Egyptian influence was earlier than Chaldaic, and Ecclesiastes, for example, is post-exilic.

(vi) Finally, we come to the longest, the most important, and the most brilliant of these fragments, the one on *The Aim of Jesus and his Disciples, with an excursus on the Resurrection*. Schweitzer's summary of this essay is well known, but I have tried to provide some more details. Footnotes to the summary are comments of mine, but I have reserved my main comment to the end.

Jesus teaches a new morality, and lays the emphasis on the next world and on judgment there. Paul says that Jesus abolished death, and Augustine holds that his great merit was to open the future life and the immortality of the soul to the ignorant. Jesus orders his Disciples to preach to the heathen instead of putting them to fire and sword as Moses did.[1]

What Jesus taught we must derive from the Gospels, which

[1] 'To the heathen'—query. See what Reimarus says below on the question of to whom the Gospel was to be preached.

agree in essentials,[1] and not from Paul or the teachings of other followers of Jesus, because their interpretation of him may be a misrepresentation.

Jesus, like John the Baptist, preached the Kingdom of Heaven, and repentance as the way to it. To the Jews this must have meant that the Messiah was coming and that his Kingdom was near at hand.

Jesus does not preach a set of doctrines, but an ethics in which it is motive and not law that dominates. 'Repent' means 'reorientate your life'. Be a better Jew than the Pharisees are. 'Love God and your neighbour' is the fulfilment of the law, but the law is not abolished.

Apart from the plain ethical commands in his teaching, Jesus remains a Jew. What he says about immortality, salvation, resurrection of the body to judgment, the Kingdom of Heaven, and the Messiah was all known to the Jews at that time. Whatever Paul did, Jesus did not teach mysteries and articles of faith.

Jesus asks for faith in himself and in the gospel, i.e. the early approach of the Kingdom of Heaven with the Messiah. Neither he nor John the Baptist explained who the Messiah was to be, or what the Kingdom and the gospel meant. All this is taken for granted to be common knowledge amongst his hearers. The Disciples are sent out to preach, but they are told nothing about what the Kingdom is or what basis the Jewish prophecies had. The Jews knew all this already. Comparisons of the Kingdom to a grain of mustard seed, a king marrying his son, hidden treasure, and so on, would leave us in the dark if we had not already known the writings of the Prophets. When Jesus shows the secrets of the Kingdom of God to his Disciples, there are no new doctrines, but only new metaphors and parables. Those who are skilled in modern catechisms and the whole apparatus of Christian doctrine read it all back into the New Testament, but it is not there. There is nothing in the teaching of Jesus about the Trinity, or about salvation through Christ as Son of God—these cardinal articles of the Church's faith.

Jesus does call himself the Son of God. But what is meant by this must be drawn from the Old Testament and not from later

[1] In a later draft, Reimarus distinguishes between John and the Synoptics. 'John's mystical Gospel puts into the mouth of Jesus his own mysterious doctrine, drawn from Cabbalists and platonizing Jews' (Strauss, *op. cit.*, p. 204). S. Neill (*op. cit.*, p. 26) attributes this distinction to F. C. Baur, but Lessing made it, and what is surprising is that it was not made long before.

doctrines. Just as in modern times a favourite youth may be called 'my son', so, in the Old Testament, Son of God means Beloved of God. Again and again men are called 'sons of God' because God loves them and they are well-pleasing in his sight (e.g. Exodus if. 22–3; Psalm ii. 7 and 12; Jeremiah xxxi. 9 and 20). The New Testament reference to 'my son in whom I am well pleased' is simply a continuation of Old Testament usage. When Jesus is tempted, Satan quotes Psalm xci. 11–12, and says 'if you are the son of God', i.e. one who trusts in him and who will be saved because God loves him, then etc. Jesus does not reply that he was born from God his Father from all eternity, and was in substance and nature alike unto him. His reply from Exodus xvi and Deuteronomy viii means that he is a man who lives on God's word and builds on God's promise, love, and care. When Jesus is mocked on the Cross ('if you are the son of God'), the reference of the mockers is to Wisdom ii. 16–18. 'Son of God' means to the Jews nothing except a pious man who loves God, obeys his commandments, and is loved in turn. So also in Matthew xxvii. 54, when those made afraid by the earthquake said 'truly this was the son of God', they meant that he was a pious man beloved of God and at whose unjust death God was enraged.

It is true that 'son of God' is also used in a special sense to apply to a greater prophet, a greater king, i.e. to the Messiah. When Jesus says that he is more than Jonah or greater than Solomon, this is just a claim to be the Messiah. But it is not a claim to be God. Jesus more often refers to himself as 'Son of Man', and he clearly teaches that the Father is greater. None is good save God only. He teaches us to pray to our Father, not to the Father and the Son, or to the Son only.

The Holy Spirit is a state of our character, the state which is well-pleasing to God. Sometimes, however, it is a synonym for God, or it may mean special gifts. People full of the Holy Spirit feel a holy urge to praise God. To baptize with the Holy Spirit is to endow with special gifts. There is nothing in all this about a concept of a special person in the Godhead.

The dove from Heaven, seen by John the Baptist alone, is just Hebrew imagery. The dove is a symbol that Jesus at baptism is endowed with unusual gifts, and not a symbol for the third person of the Trinity. If Jesus had known or wished to teach the Trinity, would the doctrine not have been taught before the Resurrection? Would the Disciples not have been taught to praise Father, Son, and Holy Spirit? We find the opposite. Jesus refuses to equal himself with God, and he never introduced a doctrine so alien to the Jews as that of the Trinity.

In St John's Gospel, there are many passages in which Jesus apparently identifies himself with God. 'I and my Father are one.' But this is simply an expression of mutual love. In the New Testament 'being at one' simply means a *consensio animorum*.

Jesus put inner conversion of heart above ceremonial laws, and meant the latter to give way, if necessary, to the former. But the laws were not abolished. Jesus 'kept the feasts', went to the synagogue, and quoted Moses and the Prophets as authoritative. The Jewish law was to be kept till Heaven and earth pass away (Matthew v. 18). Thus Jesus was a Jew who had no intention of introducing a new religion. The Disciples were not faithful to his teaching when they released Gentile converts from the Jewish law. Galatians iii. 24–5 says that the law was a schoolmaster to bring us to Christ, but we are no longer under a schoolmaster. This is to teach what Jesus did not.

Did Jesus stretch the Kingdom of Heaven beyond the Jews? He told his Disciples not to preach to Gentiles or Samaritans but only to the lost sheep of the house of Israel (Matthew x. 5–6; xv. 24).[1] But there is the curious final command after the Resurrection: Go ye therefore into all nations, baptizing them (etc.) (xxviii. 19). The instruction is strange, especially since Jesus never baptized anyone (John iv. 1–2).[2] If it was ever given, why did Peter require a vision before he was prepared to instruct Cornelius in the faith (Acts x)? If Jesus had given this instruction, why did Peter not quote it instead of relying on a vision?

This instruction has been inserted into the first Gospel (it occurs in no other) at a much later date by the Church, and the Church has altered the meaning of the Greek. In the New Testament, baptism is *into* someone's name, and it meant that the baptized person was a follower of him into whose name he had been baptized (e.g. I Corinthians i. 12–13). The Church has used 'in the name' as a formula, but it is never so used in the New Testament. The Apostles baptize 'into' the name of the Lord, i.e.

[1] This must be authentic. It could never have been invented after the Mission to the Gentiles began.

[2] Here is one of the difficulties. In John iii. 22, 26, Jesus does baptize. When did baptism begin in the Church? When it did begin, it was baptism into the name of Jesus. There is no trace in Acts of the formula in Matthew. In this passage Reimarus must be correct.

of the Messiah. The faith they require is faith in Jesus as Messiah, not as second person of the Trinity, a doctrine of which they were ignorant. If genuine, which is incredible, the formula in Matthew could only mean that the baptized was a son of God, a follower of the Messiah, and one endowed with spiritual gifts. It could not possibly mean, what the Church has made it mean, a reference to the Trinity.

The Last Supper was not the introduction of a new ritual or a new doctrine. The Passover was a memorial: the head of the house said 'this is the bread of tribulation which our fathers ate in Egypt'. The cup of red wine was also a memorial, namely of the blood shed in Egypt. Jesus is simply asking his friends to remember him at future Passover feasts. All the usual ceremonies are to be kept, but Jesus is to be remembered too until he comes again in glory, when the same feast and ritual will be continued.

The essence of the teaching of Jesus is 'repent, for the Kingdom of Heaven is at hand'. What conception of the Kingdom did the Jews have to whom Jesus spoke? To them it meant the reign of the Messiah and riddance of the Roman rule. When Jesus told his Disciples to announce that the Kingdom of Heaven was nigh, they and their listeners must have taken this to mean that the Messiah would shortly come and found his Kingdom on earth. All who took Jesus to be Messiah expected him to start to found this Kingdom. Cleopas on the way to Emmaus puts the point clearly when he says: 'We trusted that it had been he which should have redeemed Israel' (Luke xxiv. 21). What the Disciples expected during the lifetime of Jesus was temporal deliverance and a wordly Kingdom for Jews only. Only after the Resurrection did the Disciples alter the teaching of Jesus and frame a system based on a spiritual and suffering redeemer of the human race. The Gospels, written later, contain *ex post facto* material which cannot be authentic. For example, Jesus cannot have told the Disciples that he would rise the third day (Mark xiv. 28; Matthew xii. 40), for otherwise they would have expected this, instead of the reverse, as the Resurrection narratives show.

Jesus is said to have remarked: My kingdom is not of this world (John xviii. 36), but this must be a later composition, like much else in John, because it conflicts with plain facts. The ceremonial entry into Jerusalem was planned by Jesus and not inflicted on him. It could only mean that this was the coming of the Messiah, the saviour of Israel, to found his Kingdom and shake off the

Roman yoke. He goes to the Temple, chases out the money-changers, etc., and launches out against the Pharisees and the Sanhedrin. Therefore he *acts* as Messiah and Lord. When the crowd cries 'Hosanna to the son of David',[1] Jesus accepts this as a right. Unfortunately, however, it is only the crowd which accepts him as Messiah. No Pharisee or Jewish leader joined him. He had failed. He goes into hiding, but his hiding place is betrayed by Judas. He is crucified and cries out from the Cross 'My God, my God, why hast thou forsaken me?' The Kingdom which he was to have established is in ruins. The claim to be Messiah and founder of a worldly Kingdom was shattered.

The new system of the Apostles, which became the Christian religion, must rest wholly on the truth of the Resurrection, but the evidence for this is doubtful. The post-Resurrection appearances were only to the faithful.[2]

In Matthew there is a story that a Roman watch was placed over the tomb, and that after the tomb was found to be empty, the Sanhedrin bribed the watch to say that while they slept the Disciples stole the body. This is incredible. If the Sanhedrin had thought the watch worth bribing, it must have believed in the Resurrection, and this would have been evidence for the people in general. The story is never mentioned elsewhere, and it is absurd because the Roman watch could not have held its tongue, bribe or no bribe. The Sanhedrin asked for a watch on the ground that Jesus had said he would rise the third day. John says that the Disciples did not know this (xx. 9). The Disciples think, at first, that the body must be elsewhere. Matthew's story is an invention, meant to free the Disciples from suspicion of stealing the body; but it is so clearly a fabrication that it may only increase that suspicion.

The four Gospels contain such different and contradictory accounts of the Resurrection that in a court of law they would be completely discredited as witnesses. However, if the narratives do not carry conviction in themselves, may there be other evidence which requires examination?

The Old Testament does not help. In Acts, Stephen and Paul use Old Testament history and prophecy to support their belief,

[1] What does 'Hosanna' mean? In Hebrew it meant 'save now'. Modern commentators (e.g. Peake's Commentary on the Bible—revised edition, 1962—*ad loc.*) say that it had come to mean 'a shout of joy', I know not on what authority.

[2] This could be accepted only if they were different in kind from Paul's experience. See below, Chapter 8.

but there is no argument. The story of Stephen ends with a vision, but he alone saw it. The other seventy saw nothing. Paul quotes the Psalms, but they are not to the purpose: 'Thou art my son', etc., refers simply to the choice of David as King of Israel (as Psalm lxxxix makes clear), and 'see corruption' is a synonym for die (Psalm xlix. 8 and 10). Even if the quotations did refer to the coming of a Saviour, there is nothing in Paul's speech to prove that Jesus was that Saviour. Members of the Sanhedrin were scholars, who knew the Old Testament as well as anyone, yet they could not see in Jesus anything but a disturber of the peace. Were they not just as worthy of credit as the Disciples and Paul? The sign of the prophet Jonah is a curious analogy: Jonah was three days and nights in the fish's belly alive; Jesus was dead in the tomb one day and two nights. Argument from Old Testament prophecies must fail. Sometimes the sense of the Old Testament is distorted, as when Hosea xi. 1 (which refers to bringing the Israelites out of Egypt) is said to be spoken of Jesus (Matthew ii. 15). In any event, the argument from prophecy is always circular: the New Testament proves the Old one right, the Old proves that Jesus is the Messiah.

An argument from miracles fares no better. They may need as much argument themselves as what they are supposed to support. If the Resurrection took place, it needs no miracles in its support. Miracles cannot resolve the contradictions in the Resurrection and post-Resurrection narratives. It is idle to try to base faith on miracles; it is not possible to argue that because a prophet works wonders, he tells the truth. Jesus warned against miracle workers who were false Christs.

If Jesus died believing that he had failed, how did Christianity come about?

In the lifetime of Jesus, the Disciples followed him, believing that they would have thrones in an earthly Kingdom. Anything they gave up was to be repaid an hundredfold. They took the earthly Kingdom for granted, and only disputed about precedence there and raised questions about the date of its establishment. This belief was shattered by the death of Jesus.

After his arrest they all forsook him and fled. They hid until they found that proceedings were not to be taken against them. What, then, were they to do? They could not go back to their trade; they had parted with their nets and the like; they were out of practice; in any case, to go back would be to lose face; they were known as companions of Jesus.[1] So they had to be teachers. They had had experience of the standing of a teacher and of the fact that he did not starve. He received hospitality and money (e.g. Luke viii. 1–3).

What were they to teach?

First, that Jesus was the Messiah, and, secondly, the imminence of the Second Coming. Although the usual Jewish view of the Messiah was the one held by the Disciples while Jesus was alive, some Jewish sects had a different view, namely that the Messiah would come first as a suffering servant, but would return to found his Kingdom on earth. This view the Disciples now adopted. The expectation of a Messiah was strong. Two false Messiahs are mentioned in Acts (v. 36 ff.). Thus the Apostles could reckon that the many who had followed Jesus would accept this new interpretation of the Messiahship, if they could be made to believe in the Resurrection.

If the Apostles had said that the Second Coming would be delayed for centuries, they would have been mocked. No Jew expected a long period to elapse between the First and the Second Coming. Thus the Apostles had to preach an imminent Second Coming, occurring in the lifetime of many living Jews. Thus they put into the mouth of Jesus his emphatic prophecy that the Son of Man would come in glory on the clouds of heaven before the present generation had passed away. No other promise or prophecy in Scripture is so explicit.

It was not long before scoffers began to ask why the Second Coming was delayed. The word 'generation' cannot be explained away by holding that it means the Jewish people, because it does not. I Thessalonians adheres to the prophecy (iv. 13 ff.), but II Thessalonians is more obscure (ii. 2 ff.). Peter's solution is more radical: a thousand years in his sight are as one day. But what has Psalm xc to do with the matter? The words put into the mouth of Jesus are explicit.

But they have been falsified. And the Resurrection is doubtful. The few testimonies to the Resurrection are not at one in regard to any alleged post-Resurrection appearances, either in when, or how often, or to how many, or where, or about the manner of the appearances, or as to what became of Jesus at last. How could a religion rest on an incredible event to which people testify only by

[1] The spurious (?) end of John makes the Disciples fishermen in Galilee once more.

contradicting one another? Perhaps the Disciples did steal the body.

So Reimarus. What are we to make of this essay? It is so well written and so powerfully argued that the world can hardly be the same for anyone who reads it with an open mind.

Reimarus had extraordinary insight, as the following chapters will show. Again and again points arise which he had made, raised often by those who do not seem to have known his work.

His greatest merit is that he does pose clearly certain historical questions: Who was Jesus? What did he teach? How did Christianity originate? To raise the questions was the important thing, no matter what the answers. But Reimarus not only raises historical questions; he approaches them with historical imagination. New Testament phraseology has overtones resulting from its use by the Christian churches for centuries. Reimarus rightly insists on asking what it meant in the first century AD. Strauss thought that Reimarus belonged to the eighteenth century, but in fact he had the historical outlook of the nineteenth.

As for his answers, many of them have to be accepted, but there is one crucial issue on which it is not possible to follow him. He rejects the evidence for the Resurrection, but sees that he must provide some explanation of how the Disciples, after forsaking Jesus and flying into hiding, came so soon to be bold preachers of a new Gospel. What he suggests is that the Disciples at once revised their conception of the Messiah, agreed to emphasize a Second Coming which was imminent, and stole the body of Jesus in order to fabricate a Resurrection myth. Reimarus himself has pointed out (following John) that the Disciples did not expect the Resurrection. Is it credible that immediately after Jesus was buried they decided to invent one? Even if, after the Disciples fled, they remained together behind closed doors, how could they in the time available work out a new programme and execute it? Moreover, this programme involved deceit and deliberate falsehood. It is improbable that eleven men, whoever they were, could keep up a deception of this kind; one or other would have told the truth. And it is just unbelievable that these eleven were deliberate deceivers. As Schweitzer says: 'It was of course a mere makeshift hypothesis to derive the beginnings of Christianity from an imposture.'[1] The *coup de grâce* to Reimarus on this matter

[1] *Quest of the Historical Jesus* (London, 1936), p. 23.

was delivered by Goguel: '*On peut se laisser persécuter pour une illusion, mais non pour une fraude.*'[1] (One may accept persecution for an illusion, but not for a fraud.)

Nevertheless, Schweitzer's verdict on Reimarus stands: 'This was the first time that a really historical mind, thoroughly conversant with the sources, had undertaken the criticism of the tradition. . . . This essay is not only one of the greatest events in the history of criticism; it is also a masterpiece of general literature. His work is perhaps the most splendid achievement in the whole course of the historical investigation of the life of Jesus.'[2] It may be said that Reimarus had a predecessor in Spinoza, who took an historical standpoint when he considered the interpretation of Scripture in his *Tractatus Theologico-Politicus*. In Chapter VII of that work he claims that to interpret Scripture we must inquire into the historical situation in which the books were written: Who were the authors? For whom did they write, and when, and why? When was the canon settled? Spinoza illustrates his method by inquiring into the authorship of the books of the Old Testament. Often his argument reminds a reader of Reimarus, who surely derived some of his inspiration from Spinoza's book. But Reimarus goes beyond Spinoza, who did not concern himself with the historicity of the *content* of the biblical record. Reimarus did. Spinoza is one of the fathers of biblical criticism; but Reimarus is the man who challenged the historicity of the Christian religion.[3]

[1] Quoted here from H. B. Anderson: *Jesus and Christian Origins* (New York, 1964), p. 199.

[2] *op. cit.*, pp. 15, 23.

[3] J. S. Semler published a reply to Reimarus in 1779. Schweitzer thought little of it. But Dr Henry Chadwick (*op. cit.*, p. 40, footnote) describes it as very able. 'Most of the criticisms are concerned with the deficiencies of Reimarus's scholarly equipment, and it must be admitted that in this respect Reimarus delivered himself into his critic's hands at too many points.' It is to be hoped that when Reimarus is at last published entire, some competent scholar will subject his work to examination and appraisal.

CHAPTER 3

LESSING

While Lessing's publication of the Reimarus fragments may be his greatest service to theology, it was at the time less influential than some of his own writings, and I say something about a few of these, especially because of their influence on Kant and Hegel, not to speak of later writers.[1]

Although Lessing published the Reimarus fragments, he concealed their origin and authorship. If he hoped, as he alleged, that their publication would reveal to orthodox theologians the case against them, and so lead to a reply which was rationally and historically acceptable, he must have been disappointed. Those who did reply failed to rise to Reimarus's challenge,[2] and his work speedily fell into neglect. What was Lessing's real attitude? It is very difficult to give a plain answer. His work on classical philology and dramatic criticism is incisive and clear. Why is this clarity lacking in his theological writings? What did he really believe?

The answer would seem to be 'gradually less and less'. He was an opponent of orthodoxy, but was equally discontented with Deism; perhaps he was something like what in the last century has been called a Modernist, despite his repudiation of a liberal and scholarly theologian like Semler of Halle.

To the first series of the Reimarus fragments Lessing wrote a reply in 1777[3]: Whatever learned theologians may think, the Christian does not need to be bothered by the difficulties that Reimarus raises. Christianity is there for him and he feels happy in it. A paralytic helped by electrical treatment is indifferent to the truth or falsehood of theories about the nature of electricity.

In short, the letter is not the spirit; the Bible is not religion. Objections to the letter and the Bible are not objections to the spirit and religion.

Christianity was there before Apostles and Evangelists wrote, and it was a long time before the canon was settled. However

[1] My quotations from Lessing are from volumes vii and viii of the edition published in Berlin in 1956. I have made my own translations but I am much indebted to *Lessing's Theological Writings*, selections in translation, with an introductory essay by Henry Chadwick, which I have mentioned already.

[2] But see the footnote at the end of the preceding chapter.

[3] vii, pp. 812–53.

much hangs on these writings, the truth of religion cannot possibly rest on them. Christianity would remain even if they were all lost. It is true, not because Apostles and Evangelists taught it; they taught it because it is true.

After this general reply to Reimarus, which may strike a reader as somewhat cavalier, Lessing proceeds to deal with five fragments *seriatim* (those numbered, in the preceding chapter, ii, iii, iv, v, and that part of vi which deals with the Resurrection).

(ii) What Reimarus says is too one-sided. Reason, to be sure, has its part to play, but it has its limits. When it examines revelation it must be obedient to faith; this is not abdication, but recognition of limitation. Revealed religion does not presuppose a rational religion; it incorporates it in itself. Reason alone may decide whether there is or must be a revelation, but if it decides affirmatively, it must accept that there are things in revelation beyond its competence. Whoever dismisses such things from his religion has as good as no religion at all.

(iii) Yes, a revelation to all men at the same time and in the same degree may be impossible. But this does not exclude the possibility that there may be a revelation to some before others. Revelation to the Jews was the quickest way of influencing the greatest number of people. The Jews proselytized. No doubt there are objections to the Creeds and the Augsburg Confession, but Reimarus is wrong to treat them as if they were on a level with the words of Christ. It is the latter which are authorative. Reimarus's objections may touch the Lutheran system, but that is not the only Christian one.

(iv) The numbers in Exodus are not to be taken literally or as accurate. Moreover, arms of the sea vary; if one dries up, the water may flow into another with redoubled force. This may be why the Israelites went dry-shod, while the Egyptians were engulfed.

(v) Revelation is a gradual process. It is true that the Old Testament does not contain doctrines that were only learnt later, but, for all that, it provided a religion adapted to the mentality of the Jews at different times.

(vi) It is necessary to distinguish between contradictions between eye-witnesses and contradictions between accounts of what they said. Christianity conquered Judaism and heathenism, and how did this happen if the Resurrection did not happen?

Lessing was apparently writing with his tongue in his cheek, because these replies (feeble in the main) make him almost a champion of orthodoxy. Taunted with this by his brother, he replied that 'orthodoxy must be supported in order to make its downfall possible: it is patently absurd; to uphold it will hasten its destruction'. (This reminds one of Lord Clarendon on Papal Infallibility.)

Reimarus found ten contradictions in the narratives of the Resurrection and the post-Resurrection appearances, and concluded that the Resurrection never happened. J. H. Ress published a long reply in which he attempted to prove that what seemed to be contradictions were nothing of the kind. Lessing wrote a long essay (*Eine Duplik*) in reply to both Reimarus and Ress. He showed that Ress's attempt to deny the contradictions, or to explain them away, failed, but, in answer to Reimarus, he argued that contradictions affecting matters of detail in an historical record of an event could not prove that the event did not take place. (Quite so, but do the contradictions affect *Kleinigkeiten* only?)

Lessing indeed was at considerable pains to disassociate himself from Reimarus's conclusions: 'I am not pledged to the opinions of my Anonymous. I am in want of a refutation.... Here and there I can see no answer.'[1] 'Am I supposed to have brought the plague into the country because I published to the Board of Health the poison that lurked in the darkness?'[2]

Lessing asserted that the Christian religion would exist even if the Bible had never existed. This point he makes at length (*a*) in the *So-called Letters to Dr Walch* and (*b*) in his *Necessary Answer to Goeze*.[3]

(*a*) 'I maintained that objections to the Bible were not necessarily also objections to the Christian religion. The essence of Christianity can be thought perfectly well without any Bible. To a true Christian it is a matter of indifference whether a satisfactory answer to all the difficulties in the Bible can be given or not, especially if these difficulties only arise from the fact that so many sorts of writings by such different authors at such different times are supposed to form a whole in which not the slightest contradiction can be found.

'The early Christians regardep the New Testament as a *regula disciplinae*, but not a *regula fidei*. Right up to the Council of Nicaea there is no sign that the Church regarded Holy Scripture as the real source of its doctrines. At and after the Council, the Fathers

[1] *Anti-Goeze* 7, viii, 250. [2] *Anti-Goeze* 1, viii, 203.
[3] (*a*) viii, 497 ff.; (*b*) viii, 417 ff.

began to place a higher value on the Bible and gradually so represented it as if the articles of faith were and had to be derived from it. External causes must have produced this result.'

(*b*) The earliest Fathers called the content of the Creed the rule of faith. This rule is not drawn from the New Testament; on the contrary, it existed before a single book of the New Testament was written. It is older than the Church, for the rule or intention which binds a community together must precede the formation of the community. The rule of faith was regarded as sufficient for four centuries; this rule, and not Scripture, is the rock on which the Church of Christ is built. This rule was the criterion for the formation of the New Testament canon. The authenticity of the rule can be proved with far greater certainty than the inspiration of the New Testament writings can be proved, as is now supposed, by *their* authenticity. This is why modern proofs of the truth of the Christian religion are so unsatisfactory. In so far as the New Testament agrees with the rule of faith, it exemplifies it but is not its source.

Lessing derives all this from patristic writings of the first four centuries, and he supports his case by pointing out that the laity were not allowed to read the Scriptures except with a presbyter's permission, and that the early Church would never dispute with a heretic out of Scripture.

On the one hand, Lessing dismissed historical questions as being irrelevant to the Gospel, but, on the other hand, he began an investigation into the historicity of the New Testament. He had been more deeply influenced by Reimarus than he allowed his public to think. His essay *A New Hypothesis concerning the Evangelists regarded as merely Human Historians* was written in 1778, the year in which he printed Reimarus on the *Aim of Jesus*, and it must have been influenced by that essay. He sets to work as an historian. His conclusions may have been upset by later New Testament scholars, but his project was a beacon for his successors. He points out that the stories told by the Disciples must have circulated, and been embellished, before the days of printing. They were written first in Aramaic, and then translated into Greek, as Christianity spread beyond Palestine. On this foundation the Synoptists worked. The fourth Gospel was quite different. It made Christianity possible; those who knew only the Synoptic Gospels could think of Jesus as merely a human wonder-worker. This distinction between the first three Gospels and the fourth, although made almost as an afterthought by Reimarus, was an important contribution to biblical criticism. This essay was only published posthumously in 1784.

A further contribution to New Testament studies, also written in 1778 and not published until 1784, is *An Historical Introduction to the Revelation of John*. This book, Lessing says, is not mentioned in ancient literature until Justin Martyr in AD 170 (modern scholars say 136), and Justin mentions it only to support a belief in a Jubilee Year. How the book got into the canon is a mystery. (It may be a mystery still.)

In his essay on the *Education of the Human Race* (1780), Lessing makes two points which had an important influence on his successors.

The first is the unimportance of historical events for faith. Even if Reimarus were right, it would not matter. The faith does not and cannot rest on historical events. The record of these is always liable to error. Here Lessing follows Spinoza: 'Belief in historical narratives of any kind has nothing to do with the divine law. . . . It is quite untrue that belief in historical narratives is a necessary condition of our obtaining the supreme good.'[1]

This original reply to Reimarus, modified after Lessing had seen the necessity of examining the historical records if any reply were to have cogency, has had a long history. We shall encounter it in Hegel, but it comes down to my own day, for Dean Inge, who was so influential in my youth, wrote: 'How can we base our faith on the shifting sands of historical tradition which leaves us at the mercy of the good faith of reporters about whom we know little or nothing?'[2] The same view we shall encounter still more recently when we come to certain developments in modern theology. For Christianity this seems to me to be a counsel of despair, because the Christian religion, like no other, incorporates historical statements into its fundamental creed.

The startling way in which Lessing can brush history aside is clear: 'Christ was the first reliable and *practical* teacher of the immortality of the soul. Reliable because of the prophecies that appeared fulfilled in him, because of the miracles he worked; reliable by his own revivification after death. . . . Whether we can even now prove this revivification and these miracles, I set aside, just as I set aside who the person of Christ was. All that may have

[1] *Tractatus Theologico-Politicus*, ch. v and iv. Eng. tr. by A. G. Wernham (Oxford, 1958), pp. 105, 75.

[2] *Faith* (London, 1909), p. 130.

been important at that time for the acceptance of his teaching, but it is now no longer so important for recognizing the truth of his teaching' (§§ 58–9). 'Why should we not, by means of a religion whose historical truth, if you like, looks so dubious, be led to . . . better conceptions of the Divine Being, of our nature, and of our relation to God which human reason unaided could never have reached?' (§ 77).

Lessing could not make his attitude to Christianity clearer than when he said in 1777: 'Accidental truths of history can never be the proof of necessary truths of reason.'[1] The statement is unexceptionable. But it implies, in its context, that the real essence of Christianity consists of the necessary truths of reason. Reimarus again.

This is the second point which is so important for his successors. In the *Education of the Human Race* he says: 'The development of revealed truths into truths of reason is absolutely necessary if the human race is to be assisted by them. When they were revealed they were certainly not truths of reason, but they were revealed in order to become such' (§ 76). The kind of thing which Lessing had in mind may be illustrated in his fragment on *The Christianity of Reason* (published posthumously in 1784, but probably written in 1753[2]). Starting from the conception of God as *ens perfectissimum* he deduces an interpretation of the Trinity, followed by an account of the creation of higher and higher beings, culminating in the moral consciousness. God created a world in which there is a rising series of beings, each of them having some of God's perfections, and each higher one incorporating those of the lower, together with some of his own. Those beings who are aware of their own perfections and have the power of acting in accordance with them are moral beings, those who can follow a law. The moral law is "Act in accordance with your individual perfections".[3] This translation of theology into speculative philosophy is a striking foretaste of Hegel.

By evading the historical problem posed by Reimarus, and by trying to rationalize Christianity with scant regard for its historical basis, Lessing is putting the clock back. (But Reimarus did this too when he spoke of Jesus as a teacher of a purely rational religion. Reimarus the historian knew better). His attitude to history is ambivalent, as Spinoza's was. In spite of what I have quoted from

[1] *Of the Proof of the Spirit and of Power*, viii, 12.

[2] According to a note in vii, p. 861.

[3] vii, pp. 199–200.

him, Spinoza did go on to say that 'faith is based on history and language, and must be derived only from Scripture and revelation' (*op. cit.*, ch. xiv). Lessing sets history aside, and yet his essay on the *Education of the Human Race* implies the evolution of mankind, and so implicitly puts a stress on history. He does not seem to have realized this, but the nineteenth century did. The historical problem raised by Reimarus was set aside, until in the nineteenth century it was seen to be *the* problem which Christianity could not evade. Lessing, however, wrote a short note of great historical importance on the *Religion of Christ.*[1] I quote it in full:

1. Whether Christ was more than a man, that is a problem. That he really was a man if he existed at all, and that he never ceased to be a man, that is indisputable.

2. It follows that the religion of Christ and the Christian religion are two totally different things.

3. The religion of Christ is the religion which, as man, he knew and practised, which every man may have in common with him, which every man must wish to be all the more common to him, the more lofty and lovable the character which he ascribes to Christ as mere man.

4. The Christian religion is that which assumes that Christ was more than man, and makes him as such the object of its worship.

5. It is inconceivable that these two religions, the religion of Christ and the Christian religion, could subsist in Christ, in one and the same person.

6. The doctrines and principles of both religions could hardly be found in one and the same book. At any rate it is obvious that the religion of Christ is contained in the Gospels quite differently from the Christian religion.

7. The religion of Christ is contained there in the clearest and most unmistakable words.

8. But the Christian religion is there so uncertainly and ambiguously that there is scarcely a single passage which two people have ever interpreted identically.[2]

It is perhaps reasonable to infer that Lessing ultimately was far nearer rationalism than orthodoxy. At any rate, the distinctions

[1] Written probably in 1780, it was published posthumously in 1784, according to viii, 646.

[2] viii, pp. 538–9.

drawn in this note seem to me to be incontestable, although I realize that many modern theologians will maintain that the religion of Christ was a religion about him, expressed in such phrases as 'Follow thou me', 'the heart of the Gospel'.[1]

[1] M. Black in *McCormick Quarterly*, May 1967, p. 274, citing Schweitzer and Bultmann.

CHAPTER 4

KANT

Immanuel Kant was over seventy when, in 1793, he published his remarkable work on religion: *Religion within the Bounds of Reason alone.*[1] He returned to the subject five years later in his essay on the *Dissension of the Faculties.* Since these writings contain his mature views on religion, and especially on Christianity, I shall confine myself to them in the main, although I shall make some reference to his other works. My prime concern is with his conception of religion and his attitude to Christianity.

Kant was brought up in German pietism, but in later life he gave up all religious observances. He would process to the cathedral with his colleagues on ceremonial occasions, but he turned away at the door. He said that any pious and well-meaning man would be expected to fall into confusion and embarrassment if he were taken unawares when praying, or even in an attitude of prayer.[2] A religious upbringing might help to bring a child to morality, but once he discovered morality in the law of his own reason, religion ceased to be necessary for him.

In a footnote at the beginning of the *Dissension of the Faculties*, Kant says that there had been some misunderstanding of the meaning of the title he chose for his earlier work. He did not mean that religion originated from reason alone without revelation: that would have been too presumptuous; the doctrines might have originated in supernaturally inspired men. What he meant was that the revelations in the Bible could *also* be known through reason alone. Surely a student who has lived with Kant's work will take this footnote as seriously meant, and not one simply included to placate the authorities with whom he was having trouble. Kant did not reject the possibility of a revelation, but he thought that in his day any revelation that there may have been had become superfluous. This may have been derived from reflection on the doctrine of Lessing's *Education of the Human Race* (§ 4): 'Revelation gives to the human race nothing which human reason, left

[1] My page references to this work are to the translation by T. M. Greene and H. H. Hudson (Harper Torchbooks, New York, 1960). I am indebted to this work, especially to the introduction by Professor J. R. Silber, but the translation of passages directly quoted from Kant is my own. My references to Kant's other works, except where otherwise stated, are to the Insel edition, 6 vols., Leipzig, n.d.

[2] *Religion*, p. 183.

to itself, could not reach, but it just gave and gives the most important of these things earlier.'

Kant thought that the whole object of any religion which could be accepted was to inculcate or support the morality of pure reason. 'Religion is the recognition of all our duties as divine commands.'[1] What exactly does this mean? Does it mean that the categorical imperative *is* a divine command, or that those incapable of understanding the *Critique of Practical Reason* may be helped to do their duty if they think of it as a divine command? It is not easy to discover exactly what Kant's answer is. Usually he regards morality and the categorical imperative as purely *a priori*. 'Morality on its own behalf, either objectively, so far as willing is concerned, or subjectively, so far as capacity is concerned, does not need religion at all. On the strength of pure practical reason it is self-sufficient.' And yet 'since man's power does not suffice to create happiness in the world corresponding to worthiness to be happy, an omnipotent moral being must be postulated as ruler of the world, under whose providence this correspondence occurs, i.e. morality leads inevitably to religion'.[2] Moreover, 'there is one thing in our soul which, when we fix our eyes on it properly, we cannot cease from regarding with the highest wonder . . . and that is the moral disposition in us. . . . The very incomprehensibility of this disposition which *proclaims a divine origin* must work on the heart up to the point of exaltation, and strengthen it for the sacrifices which reverence for its duty may just impose upon it'.[3] But 'in religion . . . an assertion that God's existence is known is not required. . . . His existence is a problematic assumption (hypothesis) concerning the highest cause of things. . . . Faith needs only the *Idea of God* . . . without presuming ability to assure itself of the objective reality of this Idea by theoretical knowledge'.[4]

What is the religion to which morality leads and of which Kant approved? Kant bases himself on the Bible, especially the New Testament, in which he is well versed. He makes his attitude plain when he says that 'an attempt to seek in Scripture that sense which stands in harmony with the holiest thing that reason teaches must be regarded not as permissible merely, but rather as a duty'.[5] What he is after is a 'pure, and therefore universal, religion of reason'.[6] A religion can be natural and at the same time revealed,

[1] *Religion*, p. 142.
[2] *ibid.*, pp. 3–7.
[3] *ibid.*, pp. 44–5. My italics.
[4] *ibid.*, p. 142 fn.
[5] *ibid.*, p. 78.
[6] *ibid.*, p. 145.

if men could and ought to have discovered it themselves by the use of their reason, although they would not have come upon it so early.[1] This is reminiscent not only of Lessing but of Locke, who wrote: 'It is too hard a task for unassisted reason to establish morality in all its parts. . . . It is at least a surer and shorter way to the apprehension of the vulgar . . . that one manifestly sent from God . . . should . . . tell them their duties. Everyone may observe a great many truths which he receives at first from others and readily assents to as consonant to reason which he would have found hard . . . to have discovered himself.'[2] But the difference from Kant is instructive.

Once men have come upon it, Kant continues, the supernatural revelation, and the books containing it, might then be forgotten without the slightest loss to that religion.[3] In this sense the Christian religion may be regarded as a natural religion, and it is first to be examined as such.

Natural religion is morality combined with the Idea of God, as moral creator of the world, and the Idea of immortality. It is a pure practical Idea of reason, and every man can be convinced of its truth. This was what Jesus taught, and he was the first to expound this pure and searching religion.[4] It was in great contrast to the religion of the Jews who were responsive only to the incentive of worldly goods and were oppressed by burdensome rules and ceremonies characterized by external compulsion, with no consideration of the inner moral disposition.[5]

Jesus, on the contrary, claims that what makes a man well pleasing to God is not the observance of statutory ecclesiastical duties, but the pure moral disposition of the heart. It is true that he intends to retain the Jewish law, but it is obvious that the pure religion of reason must be the law's interpreter, since, taken literally, the law is the reverse of his teaching. The strait gate and the narrow way is that of good conduct; the wide gate and the broad way is the Church. Jesus sums up his teaching in two rules: Love God (the legislator of all duties) above all else, which means 'perform your duty for no motive other than immediate esteem for duty itself'; and love everyone as yourself, which means 'further his welfare from good will alone'. 'Inasmuch as ye have done it unto one of the

[1] *Religion*, p. 143.
[2] *The Reasonableness of Christianity*, Works vii, London, 1812, pp. 139–40.
[3] *Religion*, p. 144.
[4] *ibid.*, p. 146.
[5] *ibid.*, pp. 74, 116–17.

least of these my brethren, ye have done it unto me', Kant regards as a commendation of those who have helped the needy from 'pure motives of duty'. When Jesus spoke of rewards in the world to come, he did not mean to make them an incentive to action, but merely an object of the purest veneration.

Here is a complete religion which can be convincingly presented to all men through their own reason. It is made perceptible to us in the example of Jesus, but neither his authority nor the truth of his teaching requires any external certification (e.g. through miracles). There are puzzling things in this teaching, but this is because the exposition of it had to be adapted to listeners who clung to old statutory dogmas.[1] In short, the Gospel which Jesus taught was, in essence, Kantian ethics.

A religion which propounds necessary doctrines which cannot be arrived at by pure reason is a charge entrusted to the learned. The Christian faith, the basis of the Church, depends on facts and documents. These need historical and philological learning for their defence. This is unexceptionable, so long as universal human reason is the criterion of dogmatics, so that the revealed doctrine must be cherished only as a means of making the pure rational religion comprehensible. Otherwise the clergy become a tyranny over the laity, most of whom are unlearned. This is what has happened. Christianity possesses the great advantage over Judaism that it came from the mouth of the first teacher not as a statutory but as a moral religion. The Apostles did find it necessary to entwine Judaism with it. But unfortunately the Church incorporated these temporary means of teaching the moral religion into the essential articles of faith.[2] Consequently it is a duty to reform the Church; what is needed is a 'moral commonwealth' in which no yoke is laid on the multitude in the form of ecclesiastical dogmas.

On the question of the possibility of the 'moral commonwealth' Kant is an optimist, just as he was in the matter of perpetual peace. The history of Christianity, he holds, is a history of evils, and yet the Founder of the faith clearly had no other intention than to introduce a pure religious faith over which no conflict of opinion could prevail. The best period in the history of the church is the present (i.e. 1793), because the seed of the true religious faith is

[1] *Religion*, pp. 145–51.

[2] *ibid.*, pp. 151–5. See above, Ch. 2, p. 35, on 'importation'.

now being publicly sown, even though by only a few, and we may look for a continuous approximation to a Church uniting all men, which would visibly represent on earth the invisible Kingdom of God.[1] We may go further. In the end religion will be freed from all empirical grounds and from all doctrines that rest on history. Thus at last the pure religion of reason will rule over all. The history of the last two centuries provides slender grounds for Kant's optimism.

Kant's insistence that a rational faith cannot rest on historical events he shares with Spinoza and Lessing. But his depreciation of history is radical. 'The final purpose of reading the Scriptures or searching their contents is to make men better; but the historical element, which contributes nothing to this end is something in itself totally indifferent, and we can do with it what we like.'[2] Kant is not slow to follow his own prescription, when he twists sayings of Jesus into the language of the categorical imperative. He seems to take it for granted that Jesus was a purely moral teacher, and to ignore evidence to the contrary. Thus he takes issue with Reimarus (though without knowing at that date who the Fragmentist was) and insists that Jesus had no worldly design which miscarried.[3] His design was purely moral, the overthrow of a ceremonial faith and the authority of its priests, since these had crowded out the purely moral disposition.

The Bible is to be interpreted in a sense agreeing with the universal rules of a religion of pure reason. Frequently this interpretation will be forced, and yet this must be preferred to a literal interpretation which either does not help morality or may even hinder it. I should try to bring New Testament passages into conformity with my own self-subsistent moral principles.

In all religions which have sacred books, teachers of the people have expounded them in ways to bring their teaching into accordance with moral principles. For example, consider how the Greeks eventually interpreted fabulous and scandalous stories about the gods as symbolic representations of a single moral deity. Mahometans give a spiritual meaning to the sensual descriptions of paradise in the Koran. This is what must be done to the Bible, no matter how forced the interpretation is. Vengeance against enemies in the Psalms must be interpreted as war against our passions, which must be brought into subjection to reason. It is not claimed

[1] *Religion*, p. 122. [2] *ibid.*, p. 102.
[3] *ibid.*, p. 76.

that the original writers meant to write with a moral meaning, but this is how we should interpret them now.[1]

Kant fails to demonstrate the relation between this pure morality educed from the Bible and the symbolical representations in the Bible. How did the one come to be expressed by the other?

This sketch of Kant's views is drawn from *Religion within the Bounds of Reason alone*. In the *Dissension of the Faculties* his views are the same, but they are more outspoken and they are more concisely expressed. Religion, he holds, is not the sum of certain doctrines as divine revelations, but the sum of all our duties as divine commands. The difference between morality and religion is purely formal. The latter is rational legislation aimed at helping man to fulfil his duties through the rationally produced Idea of God.[2]

Doctrines are useless unless they are given a moral interpretation. The doctrine of the Trinity is of no practical use. A pupil will accept however many persons he is to worship in the Godhead, whether three or ten, because he has no conception of what 'person' means in this context, and in any case he cannot derive any rules for his life from this difference of persons. The Incarnation is the Idea, in God from all eternity, of mankind in its perfection as well-pleasing to him; but if it is regarded as Incarnation in *a* man, then this mystery can provide us with nothing practical. We cannot make ourselves like God, and *this* man could not be an example for us to follow (pp. 586–7).

It is futile to engage in learned inquiries and disputes about historical narratives in relation to religion, since the belief implanted in us by reason is sufficient by itself (p. 588).

Religion is the belief which places in the morality of man the essence of all worship of God (p. 598). The end and object of religion is to make men better morally (p. 601). The Bible has put nothing before our eyes except the incomprehensible capacity of man for morality: it points not to supernatural experiences and vague feelings, but to the spirit of Christ. Thus the biblical doctrine of faith is the true religious doctrine, grounded on the *Critique of Practical Reason*. By our reason it can be developed out of ourselves; it works with divine power on all men's hearts, bettering them, and uniting them in a universal, though invisible, Church (p. 610). Therefore there is only one religion, although there may be many faiths. Different religions have been a cause

[1] *Religion*, pp. 100–2.

[2] *Werke*, i, p. 583.

of war. But 'difference of religion'—what a remarkable expression! It is as if men spoke of different moralities.[1]

Finally, the whole is summed up as follows: Religion is purely a matter of reason. The Bible may help, properly interpreted, to spread a rational religion. God, speaking through our own practical reason, is an unerring, universally intelligible, interpreter of his word, and there cannot possibly be any other authentic interpreter. But the Bible cannot be verbally inspired. God cannot have given orders (like that to Abraham to slay Isaac) which are at variance with the moral law. To require belief in historical events is superstition. Examination of historical statements is all very well for the learned, but the aim of religious doctrine, namely to make men morally better, is missing in it, and may even be hindered by it.[2]

Kant was well taught in religion when he was young. He sometimes writes as if he were still devout. But he has reduced religion to morality and he has taken the line that, while it may help the multitude to a proper moral outlook and to an improvement of the moral life, it is unnecessary for those who, by the exercise of their reason, have come to realize what the categorical imperative is and to guide their lives by it. Worship of God is doing our duty for duty's sake. All distinctively Christian doctrines are to be jettisoned, for there is only one religion, that of universal human reason. And yet there breathes through Kant's work the spirit of religion. It is as if only a religious man could have written what he has done.

In a famous phrase Kant said that he had found it necessary to deny knowledge in order to make room for faith. In this way 'all objections to morality and religion will be for ever silenced'.[3] What, in the end, is the faith for which Kant makes room? It is at least a belief in the existence of God. It is true that this belief appears disguised as hypothesis, regulative Idea, or postulate. Kant is always cautious. But the *Critique of Pure Reason* had shown that there was nothing against the hypothesis. If the existence of God could not be proved, neither could it be disproved.[4]

'To have guidance in the investigation of nature, we must postulate a wise Author of the world.'[5] This Kant describes as a doctrinal belief, and as such it is 'lacking in stability', a somewhat

[1] *Perpetual Peace*, part ii, note 1, footnote.
[2] *Werke*, i, pp. 612–21.
[3] *K.d.r.V.*, B xxx–xxxi.
[4] *ibid.*, 669.
[5] *ibid.*, A 826–7.

mild expression of his own dismissal of the teleological argument. 'We often lose hold of it, owing to the speculative difficulties which we encounter, although in the end we always inevitably return to it.' This lack of stability, however, is absent from moral belief. In moral experience 'I inevitably believe in the existence of God . . . and I am certain that nothing can shake this belief, since my moral principles would thereby be themselves overthrown'.[1] Kant emphasizes *belief*. His moral argument 'is not intended to supply an *objectively* valid proof of the existence of God, nor to prove to a doubter that God exists'[2]; what he means is that we must *assume* the existence of God if we wish to think in a manner consistent with morality.

It may therefore not be surprising that, as was indicated above, Kant did not approve of petitionary prayer. His view is that the spirit of prayer is a heartfelt wish to be well-pleasing to God in all our actions, and this should be present in us always. But it must not be put into words or addressed to God. The Lord's Prayer expresses this spirit in a formula, the words of which can be dispensed with. Children need the words, but only as an aid to the imagination and to the quickening of a disposition to lead a life well-pleasing to God. Prayer therefore cannot be a duty for everyone. If it is thought of as an inner formal service of God, and hence as a means of grace, it is a superstitious illusion, for it is no more than a stated wish addressed to a being who needs no information about the state of mind of the petitioner. Religious services and the sacraments have no worth in themselves, though they may help to develop a pure habit of disposition if they are not regarded superstitiously, as they are if they are supposed to be 'means of grace'. The worshipper who regards the ceremonies as the whole of religion leaves it to Providence to make a better man of him, while he busies himself with piety. No mistake could be worse. The right way is not from divine grace to virtue, but from virtue to divine grace.[3]

This reference to grace may seem surprising, but in the *Critique of Practical Reason*[4] there is an interesting note comparing Christianity with Stoicism. Virtue for the Stoics was a sort of heroism in a wise man. Christians, however, seek holiness; the moral law is conceived in all its purity and strictness, and this takes away

[1] *K.d.r.V.*, A 828.
[2] *Critique of Teleological Judgment*, § 87. *Werke*, vi, 356 fn.
[3] *Religion*, pp. 183–9.
[4] Part 1, Book 2, ii, v. *Werke* v. 261.

from us all confidence that we can fully life up to it. But Christian morality enables us to hope that, if we do our best, then what is not in our power will be brought about from another source, i.e. by grace, whether or not we know how. Here there is a belief in the possibility of grace, but Kant is always clear that we can never obtain it by religious exercises, but only by obeying the moral law to the best of our ability. Compare the statement of Kirsopp Lake: 'Protestants (especially Lutherans) emphasize justification by faith as opposed to sacramental grace. . . . This doctrine insists that man can bring his life to a higher level, not by the magic of sacraments, but by an attitude of will on his own part which binds him to all that is noble in life.'[1]

For Kant, morality is always the test of religion. Religion can further morality, provided it be a pure rational religion, but it cannot contribute anything to morality. The moral law is ascertainable by pure reason, and no revelation is now necessary. The Bible is to be expounded according to morality. 'Even the Holy One of the Gospel must first be compared with our ideal of moral perfection before we can recognize him as such. . . . But how do we get the conception of God as the supreme good? Simply from the idea of moral perfection which reason delineates *a priori*.'[2] If I must know that something is a divine command before I can recognize it as a duty, then I am a devotee of revealed religion. The right way is to know that this is my duty, and then I can recognize it as a divine command. No priest is to be allowed to tell us that God requires something of us, unless we first recognize that something as a duty.[3] 'In whatever way a Being has been made known and described to us by another, yes, even if such a Being should have appeared to us (if this is possible), we must still first of all compare this image with our ideal in order to judge whether we are justified in regarding and honouring him as a divinity. Thus from mere revelation there can be no religion. The foundation *in advance* must be our concept of the [moral] ideal in its purity: that is the touchstone of any revelation. Otherwise all worship of God would be idolatry.'[4]

Although morality is the test of religion, although the aim of religion is to promote morality, the significant thing is that Kant cannot get away from religion. Morality inevitably leads to

[1] *Religion of Yesterday and To-morrow*, London, 1925, p. 32.
[2] *Grundlegung z.M.d.S.*, part 2. *Werke* v, pp. 34–5.
[3] *Religion*, pp. 142–3.
[4] *ibid.*, p. 157.

it. At the end of his life, in the *Opus Postumum*, he seems to go further than he had previously done, but this work is not a reliable guide to Kant's mature thought. Perhaps 'the categorical imperative leads directly to God, yes, serves as a pledge of his reality'.[1] Conscience is the voice of God, or almost 'the handcuff that binds us to God' (as D. M. Hay puts it in *Gillespie*). 'God is the morally practical self-legislative reason. Therefore only a God in me, about me, and over me.'[2] Here there is a hint that God is immanent as well as transcendent, and that the practical reason is the actual presence of God in man. But this is a very different view from that contained in Kant's publications. Kant's moral argument for the existence of God, based on the necessity of an ultimate happiness for the virtuous, has encountered many objections. But his ultimate thought is that the categorical imperative of duty is not intelligible except as a response to an objective moral order, and so to God and his creation. Yet his conception of God is more Judaic than Christian. His God is the transcendent creator and governor of the universe.

When he interprets the doctrine of the Trinity, he destroys all its meaning: We are to look upon the Supreme Lawgiver as (i) commanding laws appropriate to man's holiness; (ii) looking on men's moral character and only then making good their inability to fulfil the law themselves; and (iii) as dispensing a beneficence limited by being conditional on men's agreement with the holy law, in so far as, *qua* men, they could measure up to its requirement. . . . The naming of the different persons of one and the same Being expresses not inaptly the fact that God wills to be served under three different moral aspects.[3] Again, 'the highest destination (not fully reachable by men) of the moral perfection of finite creatures is love of the law. What in religion would accord with this idea is an article of faith: "God is love." In him we can revere the loving one—the Father . . .; in him also, so far as he reveals himself . . . in the archetype of humanity, engendered and beloved by him, we can revere his son; and, finally, so far as he makes his approbation of men conditional on men's correspondence with his approving love, . . . we can revere the Holy Ghost.'[4] In both of these interpretations of the Trinity, we can see the dif-

[1] Quoted here from T. M. Greene, Introduction to *Religion*, p. lxvi.

[2] Quoted from the *Opus Postumum* by N. K. Smith: *Commentary on Kant's Critique of Pure Reason*, London, 1923, pp. 639–40.

[3] *Religion*, p. 132.

[4] *ibid.*, p. 136.

ficulty which Kant has with the Third Person, and what he has to say about it remains obscure. What is not obscure is that the doctrine of the Trinity, as expounded by the Church and contained in its creeds, is one which Kant cannot accept.

Although Kant makes morality the test and criterion of religion, we must not overlook the debt which his moral philosophy owes to his religious upbringing, as we might have guessed from his insistence that what Jesus taught and revealed is just what by the exercise of our own reason we could and should have grasped. Duty for duty's sake, with its emphasis on purity of motive, is a philosophic transformation of the emphasis which Jesus placed on motive as against mere compliance with Judaic law. Why, we may ask, as we read Kant's ethical works, are human beings to be treated as ends in themselves? Is there any satisfactory answer except that Christianity has taught that every man has unique value in the sight of God, and therefore should be treated by his fellow men accordingly? The Kingdom of Ends would seem to owe its origin to the notion of the Kingdom of God on earth.[1]

Reimarus raised the historical problem in an acute form, but his work is limited by its envisaging and attacking the verbal inspiration of Scripture as a whole. Lessing, inclined to dismiss the historical problem, did see that it was necessary to scrutinize Scripture philologically, or, in other words, to re-examine the credentials of the biblical books. He did distinguish, as Reimarus had not done in the manuscript which Lessing saw, between the Synoptics and the Fourth Gospel. Kant dismisses both historical and philological criticism as all very well for the learned, but of no moral, and therefore of no religious, value. This would seem to relegate his work to a sort of backwater, which I might have omitted. Nevertheless, he had to be included for more than one reason. First, he provides one serious answer to the question which I posed: How much of Christianity can reasonably be accepted? If the answer is 'nothing, except what reason itself can excogitate', this is itself instructive, but we may venture to reject it on the ground that Kant too hastily dismissed the historical question, and so did less than justice to Christianity as an historical religion. Secondly, Kant's work made a violent impact on the young Hegel, who in turn had a profound effect on nineteenth-century theology. Hegel could not be omitted, and therefore Kant had to be included; for just as without Plato there could be no Aristotle, Hegel without

[1] Cf. H. J. Paton: *The Categorical Imperative* (London, 1947), p. 196.

Kant would have been impossible. Thirdly, Kant touched nothing which he did not adorn. He had a keen eye for essential problems and he usually went to the root of the matter. Even if, in my view, he failed to face the fundamental question, that of history, and too readily made religion the servant of morality, his writings on religion are such that no student of the subject should dare to neglect them.

CHAPTER 5

HEGEL'S EARLY THEOLOGICAL WRITINGS

To devote two chapters to Hegel may seem excessive and disproportionate, but his early writings[1] are still not well known in this country, and his later ones had an immense influence, not only in Scotland, for about forty years until Barth came on the scene. The early writings, unpublished until 1907, were prophetic. By 1800 Hegel had seized on problems that were to come to the fore in the nineteenth century.

'Religion is one of the most important concerns of our life.'[2] With that sentence Hegel begins the earliest of his unpublished writings on religious and theological subjects. It was probably written in 1793 when his course in philosophy and divinity at Tübingen ended. The sentence is certainly true of Hegel's whole life. From start to finish he is preoccupied with religion, and on religion his whole philosophy is built.

For seven years after leaving Tübingen he acted as a private tutor in Berne and Frankfurt, and it is from these years that the early theological writings are derived. They have been termed 'Anti-theological' by a scholarly critic, Professor W. A. Kaufmann, but he admits that they are not anti-religious. Certainly they are unorthodox, but only a religious man could have written them.

Kant's book on *Religion* (etc.) must have come into Hegel's hands as soon as it was published in 1793, because the influence of this book is obvious in these writings from the beginning. But although Hegel is in sympathy with Kant's rejection of orthodoxy, and agrees that learning facts and catechisms by heart is just a burden on the youthful conscience and not an aid to morality (p. 7), he has a deeper sense of what religion is. Although he quotes

[1] My translation of the more important ones was published by the Chicago University Press in 1948. It was reprinted as a paperback by Harper Torchbooks, New York, 1961, as 'Friedrich Hegel on Christianity'. On the title I was not consulted, or I would have insisted on 'Wilhelm', the name by which his sister called him, instead of 'Friedrich'. The pagination of the two editions is the same and my references are to it. When I quote from passages which have not been translated, i.e. those referred to up to p. 77, the references are to the original publication—*Hegel's theologische Jugendschriften*, edited by H. Nohl, Tübingen 1907.

[2] Nohl, p. 3.

Lessing with approval, he is turning away from the Enlightenment: 'Illumination of the intellect makes men cleverer but not better' (p. 12).

Religion is more than pure reason; it interests the heart and influences our feelings. It gives a new and sublimer impetus to morality and its motives (p. 3). If religious doctrines are to be effective in life and action, they cannot be built on reason alone (p. 14). The people most worthy of respect are certainly not always those who have speculated most on religion, and who very often turn their religion into theology. Religion gains little from the intellect, whose activities and doubts may cool the heart rather than warm it. The essence of religion is missed by those who pride themselves on having risen above the absurdities of the heathen. The man who calls his Jehovah 'Jupiter' or 'Brahma', and who is a true worshipper of God, gives thanks and makes his offering with as much simplicity as a true Christian (p. 10). To say that a man has religion does not mean that he has great knowledge, but that his heart feels the acts, the miracles, the nearness of divinity; he recognizes and sees God in nature, in the fate of men; he prostrates himself before God, thanks him and praises him; he does not simply consider whether his action is good or clever, but the thought that the action is well-pleasing to God is a sufficient motive for doing it (p. 6). In all this Hegel is following and yet beyond Kant. He has seen more deeply into the religious consciousness, just because he was and remained a more religious man than Kant was himself.

Hegel distinguishes between objective and subjective religion. The former is a faith made into a system and contained in books. Intellect and memory are the forces operative in formulating and spreading it. Subjective religion, however, is a thing of the heart. The problem is to make objective religion subjective; and, in particular, to construct a national religion (*Volksreligion*) which is neither a purely rational religion nor fetishism or superstition. It is important to draw mankind towards a rational religion. Here Hegel follows Kant. But a universal spiritual Church remains a mere ideal of reason, and it is hardly possible to establish a public religion from which no fetishistic faith whatever could be derived. Hence the problem is how to set up a national religion which will avoid superstition so far as possible and at the same time lead the nation towards a rational religion (pp. 17–20).

There are two points of importance in this conception of the religion of a folk, people, or nation. The first is that religion is not a purely private or individualistic matter. It is social. The second is that the religion of a people is bound up with the rest of its civilization. Religion has an essential part to play. 'The spirit of a people, its history, its religion, its degree of political freedom, can neither be considered by their influence on one another nor by their separate characteristics. They are woven together in one bond of connection' (p. 27). This is the beginning of Hegel's historical insight.

In a national religion (i) the doctrines must be founded on universal reason. This is Kant. But (ii), and this is what Kant did not see so clearly, imagination, the heart, and the senses must nevertheless not be sent empty away. And (iii) all the needs of life and the public acts of state must be connected with it. On the other hand, superstition is to be avoided; the demand of reason is not satisfied by tirades about illumination and so forth; and we are not constantly to be at loggerheads about dogmatic doctrine, a procedure that makes no one any better (pp. 20–1). Kant had said the same.

(i) The rational doctrines must be simple, not requiring any apparatus of learning, and they must be human, i.e. adapted to that level of morality which a people has reached. Some of the loftiest doctrines can be the property of men brought to wisdom by long experience. One of these is the doctrine of God's providence, with which complete devotion to God is bound up. But, in plenty of people, belief in this doctrine can be destroyed by a shower of rain or a bad night. This is what comes of trying to tie the belief to facts instead of exhibiting it as necessarily connected with our morality and our conception of the holiest.

With this doctrine of providence, as it is commonly expounded, it is instructive to compare the faith of the Greeks, especially their notion of fate. This notion reverences natural necessity; it involves the conviction that man is ruled by the gods in accordance with moral laws; therefore it is adapted to the sublimity of the divine and to man's weakness, his dependence on nature, and the restricted range of his vision (pp. 20–2).

(ii) Ceremonies are essential. Even a rational religion needs a body. It is a good thing to tie myths to religion in order to prevent venturesome excesses of imagination. Most Christian doctrines are tied to history or presented through it, and this sets to imagination an easily recognizable limit, but we are too much men of reason and of the letter to love beautiful images, like those of Greece (pp. 23–4).

(iii) If a wall is built between doctrine and life, religion fails. There is too much emphasis on the letter; too many bigoted demands are made, and men's natural needs are opposed. Religion ought to promote joy and not negate it, to promote festivals and not discourage them. All the Greek festivals were religious. Alas! the Greek spirit of joy and beauty has fled. The Greek youth were not fed on the bitter sweets of mysticism but on the milk of pure feeling (pp. 26–9).

Here the fragment ends. It is a mistake to suppose that Hegel wishes to bring Greece back. He knows that that is impossible. His problem is: Can we revivify our religion and give it some of the joy and beauty of the Greek? Can we free it from all the paraphernalia of orthodox dogmatics and so make it a living moral force in national life?

The remaining four fragments to which Nohl gave the general title *National* [*Volk*] *Religion and Christianity* contain a formidable indictment of orthodoxy. Most of the material in them either repeats things mentioned already, or anticipates the later essay on the *Positivity of Christianity*. But there are some points which deserve special notice, indicative as they are of Hegel's views on Christianity at this date in his life, i.e. when he was about twenty-four.

Man's highest aim, he argues, is moral, and amongst his aptitudes for furthering it one of the chief is religion. The aim of religious institutions is not merely the promotion of morality through the Idea of God, but of morality in general. This it does by doctrines and ceremonies. How effective are those of Christianity?

Originally Christianity was a private religion, i.e. for small groups of individuals, though, owing to the circumstances of its origin, there were other elements in it. (*a*) Its practical doctrines are pure, i.e. rational and not arbitrary. It exhibits goodness mostly in examples; in the Sermon on the Mount the spirit of morality is portrayed in universal terms. But it does not restrict itself to form alone: it contains material prescriptions, and this has led to misunderstandings. (*b*) The miraculous element in the historical statements on which it is built is always open to unbelief. (*c*) Its ceremonies, appropriate in a private religion, have lost their meaning, and are subject to endless and futile disputes, now that it has become a public religion (p. 49).

Attempts to show that the positive doctrines of Christianity are, though above reason, not contrary to it do not get very far, because reason is the supreme judge of what reason believes. We might say that the doctrines are not contrary to reason, but that it is contrary to reason to believe them (pp. 53–4).

If you write about the Christian religion, you will be met by a critic who objects to your account of it and asks if you have read his summary. These summaries are so divergent that they must be ignored. We must go to the New Testament (pp. 60–1).

Of great *practical* importance, unlike most orthodox doctrines, is the history of Jesus himself, not just his teaching or that ascribed to him. He was not simply a man who developed his ideas in solitude, then devoted himself entirely to the bettering of men, and ultimately gave his life for this end. This would merely put him on the same footing as Socrates. Without the divinity of his person we would have only a man. As it is, he is a true superhuman ideal of virtue (p. 56). Belief in Christ is belief in a personified ideal (p. 67), as Kant had almost said.[1] This ideal is no cold abstraction; it is individualized, heard speaking and seen acting. He is not just a virtuous man, but virtue itself, without blemish and not disembodied.

What has happened? John the Baptist said 'Repent', Jesus 'Repent and believe the Gospel', the Apostles 'Believe in Christ'. Taught by them we concentrate on the death of Christ, as if others had not died for less. Missionaries spread his name, so that the line they take diverts attention from the moral teaching. The result is a faith dependent on memory, sparing of good disposition and good actions, preached on the Ganges and the Orinoco to people who already have a faith adapted to their needs.

Faith in Christ as an historical person is not grounded in a need of practical reason. It is a faith resting on the testimony of others. A faith based on reason is open to anyone who will listen to reason's voice. An historical faith, on the other hand, is restricted in its appeal. It is a well on which not everyone can draw, although theologians (as Kant had complained) make its acceptance a condition of salvation. Either, therefore, most of the human race are excluded from salvation (as some believe), or this faith has not the enormous importance claimed for it (pp. 64–5).

To find the truly divine in Jesus is not to find it in his being the second person of the Trinity, begotten of the Father from all

[1] *Religion*, pp. 55, 120.

eternity, but in the fact that his spirit coincided with the moral law. This is what theologians have misconceived and misrepresented (p. 67).

Finally, the Christian religion, always throughout its history coloured by its time and by political conditions, is now at last acquiring its own true independent dignity: i.e. its rational centre is being emphasized, its doctrines, especially those resting on historical statements, discarded (p. 71). This is reminiscent of Kant, who thought that the late eighteenth century was the best age in the history of the Church.

If we put to Hegel at this stage in the development of his thought the main question with which we are concerned, namely: How far can reason take us on the road to Christian belief?, his answer is not quite the same as Kant's. Like Kant he believes that Jesus taught nothing but pure morality, although his conception of morality has more room for the heart and the feelings than Kant's had. With Kant, again, he discards most theological doctrines, and rests faith entirely on reason and especially not on historical events. But, attaching more importance to religion than Kant does, and seeing it as one essential strand in national life, he asks how Christianity can be modified in order to make it a vital force and an aid to the betterment of mankind.

It is at this point, however, that Hegel sees that history cannot be so readily dismissed. In three long essays he devotes himself to the problem of Christian origins. The first essay is a life of Jesus[1] sub-titled 'Harmonization of the Gospels after my own Translation'. Lives of Jesus have been common enough since, but in 1795 Hegel had hardly any predecessors. This is what gives the essay its importance.

No work of Hegel's is so perplexing as this. Kant had argued that Jesus taught the morality of the categorical imperative, and he provided examples of how to interpret some Gospel sayings in this sense. Even if the interprettion were forced, it was a duty to make reason the interpreter. Hegel takes this duty on himself and works out in detail these Kantian views. He took great pains; the surviving manuscript, unlike others, has hardly any erasures, so that he seems to have gone to the trouble of making a fair copy of an earlier draft.

The basis of his 'harmonization' is the Gospel of Luke; miracles

[1] There is a French translation (by D. D. Rosca, Paris, 1928), but, so far as I know, no other.

are not mentioned; Jesus was born of Joseph and Mary in Bethlehem; the life ends with his death. In this there is nothing remarkable or surprising, given the date of composition. What is surprising is the exegesis. None could be more 'forced'.

Hegel begins by interpreting as follows the beginning of the Fourth Gospel: 'Pure reason, free from all limitations, is the Godhead itself. Thus it is in accordance with reason that the whole plan of the world is ordered. It is reason which teaches man his destiny and an unconditioned aim of his life. Reason is often darkened, but never altogether obliterated; even in darkness a weak glimmer of it is always retained' (p. 75).

A few further examples may best convey the flavour of the whole: St Matthew says 'All things whatsoever ye would that men should do to you, do ye even so to them: for this is the law and the prophets' (vii. 12). Hegel translates: 'Make the maxim of your will that what is to be a universal law for mankind is to be valid for you too; this is the fundamental law of ethics' (p. 87).

'Think not that I have come perhaps to preach the invalidity of the laws or to cancel their obligatoriness: I am come to complete them, to breathe life into this dead carcase. Heaven and earth may well pass away, but not the demands of the moral law or the duty to listen to them. . . . What I add, in order to fulfil the whole system of the laws is the prime condition that you are not to be satisfied with observing the letter of the law . . . but that you act in the spirit of the law out of reverence for duty' (pp. 82–3).

'The word of God' (in the parable of the sower) becomes 'knowledge of the moral law' (p. 92).

'If you take your ecclesiastical statutes and positive commands for the supreme law given to man, you misconceive the dignity of man and his capacity to draw out from himself the conception of God and knowledge of his will. Whoever does not honour this capacity in himself does not honour God either' (p. 89). The last phrase is supposed to be the exegesis of 'He that honoureth not the Son honoureth not the Father'.

'Do you suppose that God has thrown the human race into the world and abandoned it to nature, without a law, without a consciousness of the end and aim of its being, without the possibility of finding *within* the way to be well-pleasing to God? . . . I cling solely to the pure voice of my heart and conscience. . . . To listen to its voice is what alone I demand of my disciples. This inner law of freedom to which, as given by himself, man submits freely'

(p. 98). Thus is explained 'Ye shall know the truth and the truth will make you free'.

'I thank thee, Father, that to know what constitutes each man's duty is not a matter of learning and erudition, but that every uncorrupt heart can feel for himself the difference between good and evil. Would that man had stopped at this and not, in addition to the duties which reason imposes, manufactured a mass of burdens to plague poor humanity with' (p. 102).

'Men have been given the law of their reason. Neither from heaven nor from the grave can any other teaching be given, because any such would run counter to the spirit of that law which requires an obedience which is free, not one slavish or one extorted by fear' (p. 111–12).

It would be tedious to quote further examples of this forced attempt to make Jesus an expositor of the *Critique of Practical Reason*. It is fair to add, however, that the narrative is carefully constructed with great skill; except when a reader is put off by Kantian expressions, it is also moving. Distorted though the narrative be, it does nevertheless bring home to the reader that it describes the life of no ordinary man.

What are we to make of it? What was Hegel's intention in composing it? It might be thought that he was simply testing in detail the suggestions he had learnt from Kant, but there is one feature of the essay which seems to me to make this very unplausible. This is the inclusion of explanations which ignorant readers might be thought to require. John the Baptist fed on locusts, which, Hegel adds, are edible in those parts. The Disciples plucked ears of corn, or, Hegel says, whatever other plants they may have gathered, perhaps oriental beans. A parable, Hegel explains, is a narrative exhibiting a certain doctrine in a sensuous form. In a parable the agents are men; this distinguishes it from a fable, where the agents are animals, and a myth, where the agents are demons or allegorical beings. The Pharisees and Scribes are those in whose hands the government of the country rested. Jesus rode on an ass; this was the practice in the east. Jesus distributed bread; this accorded with the custom of the east, just as today among the Arabs eternal friendship is cemented by eating the same bread and drinking from the same cup. The crown of thorns consisted of the plant *Heracleum*, acanthus. Crucifixion was a Roman punishment, as dishonourable as a death on the gallows is today.

If Hegel had been writing for himself alone, these parentheses were unnecessary. It would seem therefore that what he was trying to do was to produce scriptures for the sort of rational Christianity which his earlier papers had envisaged.[1] Whether this be so or not, it did not take him long to see that this life of Jesus would not do. It was not history.

Hegel's study of the Gospels owes nothing to Lessing's attempt to put them in order, or to dinstinguish between the Synoptics and John. He takes his material from all four Gospels and tries, indeed, to harmonize them. Thus he is still at the standpoint of the early Reimarus, so far as the scriptures are concerned, but he is not yet the historian that Reimarus is. Nevertheless, he does now see that there is an historical problem. If the teaching of Jesus was in fact what Hegel had represented it to be, how could the Christian religion, in its orthodox form, ever have arisen? If Jesus taught pure rationality, how did the Christian religion depart from this and become 'statutory' (to use Kant's word—he had seen the problem too) or 'positive' (to use Hegel's)? 'Positive' is a term adopted as a contrast to 'natural' or 'purely rational'. It means 'laid down', not deduced from pure reason alone. A 'positive' religion is one grounded on authority, and it puts man's worth not at all, or at least not wholly, in morality.[2] It is obvious today that, in this sense, Christianity is a 'positive' religion. How did it become so? How has it become what it is? It is to these historical questions that Hegel addresses himself as soon as he has finished his life of Jesus in 1795.

The second of the long essays to which I referred is on *The Positivity of the Christian Religion*. Most of it is devoted to an attack on the Church. Schiller said that toil was needed to get at the well-spring of truth, but the Church offers truth in the open market. The stream of ecclesiastical truth gurgles in every street. The dispensers of this flood are the Church's officials (p. 134). By thus ignoring the rights of reason, the Church has distorted a gospel of freedom and made it a tyranny over the laity. Again and again Protestants have appeared and tried to get back to freedom, but they have formed sects, and these have lapsed into tyrannies once more. This polemic, which smacks of the *Aufklärung* or Voltaire,

[1] This, I now find, is also the view of Professor Kaufmann: 'Surely this is Hegel's attempt to write the scriptures of his folk-religion' (*From Shakespeare to Existentialism*, Boston, 1959, p. 131).

[2] P. 71. From this point until the end of this chapter the page references are to the English translation.

need not concern us. It is the historical passages which are more interesting and important for our purpose.

Hegel holds that the foundation for all judgments on the Christian religion is that the aim and essence of all true religion is human morality. There can only be one true religion, namely natural religion, the one adapted to our human nature and derived from reason. (This, as we have seen, is Kant.) The object which Jesus had in view was to raise religion to morality and to restore to morality the freedom which is its essence. This was very remarkable, because Jesus was a Jew, and only by considering the essence of Judaism is it possible to understand what Jesus was attacking. The Jews were overwhelmed by a burden of divine statutory commands which pedantically prescribed a rule for every casual action of daily life and gave the whole people the look of a monastic order. They had done their duty when they had compiled with the rule, or, in other words, they substituted legality for morality. This was what Jesus opposed with all his strength. He tried to show how little the observance of the Mosaic law constituted the essence of virtue, since that essence is the spirit of acting from reverence for duty, first, because it is a duty, and, secondly, because it is also a divine command. (The influence of Kant is still obviously strong.)

The Jews were so certain that their entire polity had divine authority that it was useless to appeal to reason alone in preaching to them. Jesus had to claim authority for his teaching. Therefore he demands attention to his words, not because they are adapted to the needs of our spirit, but because they are God's will. He may have held that the law hidden in our hearts was an immediate revelation of God or a divine spark, and his certainty that he taught only what this law enjoined may thus have made him conscious of a correspondence between his teaching and the will of God.

The Jews expected a Messiah, and from him they might have been disposed to accept new teaching. Hence the Disciples accept the teaching of Jesus, thinking that he is the Messiah. Jesus could not exactly contradict them, for otherwise he had no hope of making an entry into their minds. But he did try to lead their messianic hopes into the moral realm.

Some attention Jesus received on the score of the miracles attributed to him. What is of importance is not to speculate on their historicity, but to realize that these deeds of Jesus were miracles in the eyes of his Disciples and friends. This increased his authority in their eyes and helped to make them interpret as statutory what was not meant to be.

The final command given by Jesus to his Disciples, as reported in Mark, so different from the valedictory discourse in John, is characteristic of a teacher of a 'positive' religion, because it places all value on believing, instead of on doing.

Thus, although the teaching of Jesus requires an unconditional and disinterested obedience to the will of God and the moral law, it contains these other features which induced his followers to base knowledge of God's will, and the obligation to obey it, solely on the authority of Jesus. Even moral doctrines, now made obligatory, not on their own account, but because commanded by Jesus, lost the inner criterion whereby their necessity is established, and they were placed on the same level with every other 'positive' command and external ordinance. Thus the religion of Jesus became a '*positive*' doctrine about virtue.

Socrates did not care how many disciples he had. Jesus limited the number to twelve. 'The result of restricting the highest standing to a specific number of men . . . led eventually to the episcopate and to Councils of clergy who, by a majority vote, imposed their decrees on the world as a norm of faith' (pp. 82–3).

'Christianity has emptied Valhalla . . . extirpated the national imagery as a shameful superstition . . . and given us instead the imagery of a nation whose climate, laws, culture, and interests are strange to us and whose history has no connection whatever with our own. . . . Is Judaea then the Teutons' fatherland?' (pp. 146–9).

In this essay Hegel is beginning to be an historian. It is free from the distortions of the life of Jesus. Nevertheless, it is still untouched by biblical criticism. There is no sign that Hegel ever read Reimarus. If he did, he simply ignored him. However, the important thing is Hegel's growing historical insight, evidenced above all in the section which describes how Christianity conquered Greco-Roman paganism (pp. 151–64). He dismisses the usual explanations, as, for example, that acquaintance with Christianity made people dissatisfied with their fabulous mythology and ready to accept what was adapted to both heart and reason and which had a divine origin authenticated by miracles. This suggestion that men became so 'enlightened' that they exchanged paganism for Christianity will not survive the 'simple observation that the heathen too had intellects'. The supersession of a native and immemorial religion by a foreign one is a revolution whose causes must be found in the spirit of the times. Greco-Roman religion was a religion for free men, for republics. When freedom disappeared from public life, the old religion disappeared too, and this is why Christianity was received and accepted.

Whatever may be thought of Hegel's answers to the historical questions which he raised, he must be given credit for raising them, and some at least of his points seem valid. Surely he is right to begin any quest for Christian origins by examining Judaism and considering the beliefs of the Jews to whom Jesus spoke. Surely he is right again to regard religion as part of the spirit of the age, and subject to change as the spirit changes. Is this not an important reflection for us today, when so many of the strands of our life are so different from what they were in Victorian times, and when the religion which was so vigorous and which played such an important part in life then, has now so visibly lost its hold on so many of our contemporaries and juniors?

On many other points we may think Hegel wrong. If so, we are in agreement with him. He was his own best critic. Four years after writing this essay he rewrote the first few pages of it, and on many crucial points he had completely changed his mind. He had still further deepened his historical sense.

Hegel now says (pp. 167–81) that to suppose that there is one true religion, natural religion, the one adapted to human nature, is a mistake, because there is no such thing as unvarying human nature. What is real is always some modification of 'human nature', and the modification is perhaps the only thing which is 'natural and beautiful'. A religion adapted to one culture may be natural there, but, continuing in a different culture, it may then become merely 'positive'. Enlightened people characterize our religion as empty superstition, deception, and stupidity, a relic of the Dark Ages, untenable in an enlightened age. But this does not explain the construction of a fabric so apparently repugnant to reason. Church history is appealed to and it is made to show how simple and fundamental truths become gradually overlaid with a heap of errors. This method of explaining the matter, however, presupposes a deep contempt for man and the presence of glaring superstition in his intellect; it takes religion in abstraction from the life of the time, to the needs of which it has been appropriate. Man's nature always and necessarily has religious feeling as one of his higher needs, and the system of his faith can never have been stupidity unalloyed. Man has a natural consciousness of a supersensible world and an obligation to the divine. Everything high, noble, and good in man is divine; it comes from God and is his spirit. This view becomes positive only if human nature is severed from the divine, if no mediation between the two is conceded except in one isolated individual, and if our consciousness of the divine is degraded to the killing belief in a superior Being altogether alien to man. (As my readers will realize, all this seems to me to be true.)

Hegel the historian now seeks to understand instead of to condemn. His picture of Jesus is now far more historical than the one he painted in the *Life*, and it is far more sympathetic than it was in the early writings on National Religion and Christianity. He has also come to stress the importance of the doctrine of the Holy Spirit, and he sees that it presents him with the philosophical problem of the relation between finite and infinite. He is now prepared to pull together all the threads of his theological studies by making up his account with Christianity. This he did in the third of the long essays to which I referred, the brilliant, but often perplexing, essay to which Nohl gave the title *The Spirit of Christianity and its Fate* (pp. 182–301).

Hegel begins with a remarkable analysis of Judaism and its fate. It is a grim indictment. Abraham strikes the keynote by tearing himself away from all his kinsfolk; the bonds of communal life and love are snapped. The world he sees as sustained by God, but God is alien to it; nature has no part in God but is under God's mastery. The Jews believe themselves to be a chosen people; they cut themselves off from other peoples; assured food, drink, and progeny are God's claims to their veneration; as the title to veneration, so the veneration, the former, relief of distress, the latter, bondage.

Somewhat unwillingly they were freed from bondage in Egypt by Moses, but he freed them from one yoke by laying on them another—the Mosaic law. The Jews could not surmount their fate or extricate themselves from it. It was their fate to submit to their fetters and persist in their exclusiveness and their hatred of the Gentiles.

While the truth in this account cannot be gainsaid, it is nevertheless very one-sided. Hegel has nothing to say about the religious genius of the Jews, as evidenced in the Psalms and the Prophets. He does not mention the former, and he reduces the latter to fanatics.

However, he may be right when he says that what Jesus opposed was the legality which seemed to satisfy the Jews. Obey every jot and tittle of the law, and then you will have the support of God in heaven. God is always *there*, and never in the heart. Jesus, on the contrary, preaches the precedence of the heart over the law. To obey the law is something, but everything depends on motive or on the spirit in which the law is obeyed. This was to oppose the whole of the Jewish fate. But enmities like those which Jesus sought to transcend can be overcome only by valour. They cannot be reconciled by love. Jesus was therefore bound to fail and to be a victim of the fate which he had tried to defeat. This is why his religion has had a great reception, not amongst his own people, but in the rest of the world.

In outlining the moral teaching of Jesus, Hegel begins by parting company with Kant. He has travelled a long way in the few years since he wrote his life of Jesus. 'We might have expected Jesus', he says, 'to work against legalism, bondage to positive or statutory commands, by showing that moral commands were grounded in the autonomy of the human will. But this puts inclination and feeling in bondage to reason, so that the moral man is a slave of himself, just as the Jew was a slave to the law. One who wished to restore man's humanity in its entirety could not possibly have taken a course like this. To act in the spirit of the law could not have meant for him "to act out of respect for duty and to conquer inclination", for that only produces distraction of soul along with an obdurate conceit.'[1] Jesus thus goes beyond morality (or at least Kantian morality) as well as legalism, and teaches a solution of inner conflict by religion. He came to 'fulfil' the law, by requiring a righteousness other than that of the Scribes and Pharisees: in a religious disposition, the opposition between inclination and law disappears. The correspondence of the two is life and love. In love all thought of duties vanishes. Just as virtue is the complement of obedience to law, so love is the complement of the virtues. For the multiplicity of the virtues, love substitutes a living spirit which will express itself, not in rules or generalizations, but appropriately on every different occasion for action. It will never have the same shape twice. It overcomes the notion of pure objectivity. Love, whether of God or my neighbour, is the sensing of a life similar to my own. Teaching of this kind is to the Jews the most incomprehensible opposite of the Jewish spirit.

[1] For my comment on this passage, see *Action* (London, 1968), pp. 228–9.

The religious teaching of Jesus was just as much opposed to Jewish ideas. To the Jewish idea of God as their Lord and Governor, Jesus opposes a relationship of God to men like that of a father to his children. Love itself is still incomplete in nature; religion is its fulfilment because religion is reflection and love united. The divine is pure life, and its activity is a unification of spirits. Only spirit grasps spirit in itself. Unfortunately Jesus had to use the language of objectivities and matters of fact, and the phrases he uses seem harsh: I am the true bread; entry into the Kingdom of Heaven, etc. This is what has led to so much misunderstanding. Father and son are simply modifications of the same life, and therefore if God is our father, there is something of divinity in man. Faith in the divine is only possible if in the believer himself there is a divine element.

It is true that, in many of the discourses in John, Jesus claimed to be an individual with special characteristics of his own, not shared by other men. But this was only to contrast himself with the Jews, from whom he did claim to be distinct in spirit. In so far as Jesus claimed divinity or oneness with God, this was something that all the children of God could have also, if they were animated by the Holy Spirit and so sharers in the divine life. It is a mistake to try to find the essence of Jesus in some exceptional individuality or personality.

Jesus completed the religion, as he founded it, with the conception of the Kingdom of God. The use of the word 'Kingdom' calls up false associations. What Jesus meant was a living harmony of men in fellowship with God: not a collection of men, but a communion unified by life and love.

This exegesis of the teaching of Jesus has much more historical plausibility than the earlier *Life*, and most of it I accept. It will be noticed, however, that the picture of Jesus is that of a man who is an inspired teacher, no more. Moreover, here too, as in his previous essays, Hegel takes no interest in biblical criticism, and therefore he does not raise many of the historical problems posed by later work in that field. The concluding passages of the essay are, however, of striking importance.

The teaching of Jesus was addressed to individuals. Precepts like 'sell all you have and give to the poor' cannot be of universal application. What Jesus sought to found was a loving community, not a Church.

What happened? A loving circle, like that of the Disciples, is a

Kingdom of God on a small scale. But their love is not yet religion, because for religion there must be an objectification of the oneness of the group. If the divine is to appear, the invisible spirit must be united with something visible. Otherwise there remains the quenchless unsatisfied thirst after God. When Jesus died, the Disciples were like sheep without a shepherd. Their faith in pure life had hung on the individual Jesus; in him God had appeared to them. What then was wanting in the community's life was an image and a shape. In the risen Jesus, in love thus given shape, the need for religion finds its satisfaction.

To consider the Resurrection of Jesus as an event is to adopt the outlook of the historian, and this has certainly nothing to do with religion (p. 292). Nevertheless, history cannot be set aside altogether. The divinity of Jesus is the deification of a man who lived and taught and died as a man, as an historical character. Thus the image of the risen one has appended to it a mundane reality hanging on the deified one and dragging him down to earth. It is not the risen one alone who is the cure of sinners and the ecstasy of their faith; prayers are also offered to the man who taught and who hung on the cross. The community cannot renounce the conception of natures of two different kinds. It is over this tremendous combination that, for so many centuries, millions of God-seeking souls have fought and tormented themselves.

The form of a servant, as the veil of divine nature, would present no obstacle to the urge for religion if only the real human form had been satisfied to be a mere veil and to pass away. But this real human form is supposed to remain fixed and permanent in God. Consquently, the Christian community's spirit was not completely manifested in love configurated, in the risen Christ: it demanded manifestation in the real individual, Jesus, and so in a Lord and Master. It recognized its real bond in common dependence on a common founder and in an intermixture of history with its life. This insistence on mundane reality caught the community in the toils of fate.

When worship is demanded for Jesus the man, he never becomes divine, whatever radiance may shine around him. It is true that there are stories about his birth and transfiguration, but the heavenly phenomena 'which surround the individual, and whose divinity is greater than his', only serve to emphasize his humanity.

Miracles, which we cannot accept, were believed to be miracles by the Apostles, because they did not so clearly distinguish spirit and body as we do; prophecies prove nothing, except where it is possible to discern a similarity of spirit between them and Jesus.

By conjoining the man Jesus with the deified and glorified Christ, the Apostles were seeking to satisfy the deepest urge for religion. This was because their consciousness hovered between reality and spirit. They failed: they pined for union with the risen Lord, but this was eternally impossible because he remained for them an individual, a human person. This has been characteristic of the history of Christianity. It is contrary to its emotional character to find peace in a non-personal living beauty, and therefore it has been tormented by oppositions throughout its history. The divine and the human are never reconciled. It is the fate of Christianity that Church and State, worship and life, piety and virtue can never melt together into one.

With this essay, whatever we may think of it, Hegel took immence pains. A number of earlier partial drafts have been printed, and even so his final manuscript is full of erasures. He begins as an historian by placing Jesus in the context of his time. He shows what it was in Judaism that Jesus was reacting against. He expounds the teaching of Jesus, showing that the moral and religious teaching are not distinct; on the contrary, it is religion as love which he substitutes for Kant's ethics. This all seems sound, but there is insufficient appreciation of the importance of Judaic Messianism for Jesus and the Disciples (perhaps because it no longer has importance for Hegel—or for us).

It is clear that he rejects all the miracles as non-historical, and yet he ascribes some sort of value to them on the ground that the Apostles believed in them. If we ask how far he accepts the creeds of the Christian Church, we have no very precise answer. Certainly he rejects them if they are taken literally. The doctrine of the Trinity, for example, is explained as describing three stages in man's religious development (p. 273). Perhaps the outcome is that, at this stage, like Lessing, he accepts the religion of Jesus, as he interprets it, but not the Christian religion.

Although it looks as if, with this essay, Hegel had settled his attitude to Christianity, this is not really his last word on the matter. It is necessary to glance at his philosophy of religion and his treatment of Jesus in his later writings.[1]

[1] In the Prefatory Note to my translation of Hegel's *Early Theological Writings*, which was dated November 1, 1946, I said that I hoped to produce a book on the development of Hegel's thought. This hope was vain. Two-thirds of the book were written but, first, other preoccupations, and now, personal circumstances, make it impossible for me to complete it. A great deal of new material has appeared since 1946, especially the four volumes of Hegel's letters, not to speak of the volumes of *Hegel Studien*, and what I have written would have to be radically revised. Much of the new material has been used by Mr G. R. G. Mure in his *Hegel* (London, 1965), and to still greater extent by Professor Kaufmann in his *Hegel* (New York, 1965). These works, and especially the latter, have made the completion of my book, even if it had been possible, unnecessary. In my opinion, Professor Kaufmann overestimates the importance of the fragments written before the *Life of Jesus*, and seriously underestimates the essay on the *Spirit of Christianity*, but he has done more than even Lukács to unravel the early development of Hegel's thought.

CHAPTER 6

HEGEL'S LATER THEOLOGICAL WRITINGS[1]

In the last chapter we saw Hegel beginning by contrasting Christianity with Greek religion. The latter was happy and beautiful; it was tied in with public life; all the great festivals were religious. Christianity, on the other hand, had arisen out of misfortune (the subjection of the Jewish people to Rome) and was for those in misfortune (for those who had lost their freedom under the Roman Empire). But this gloomy Christianity was not the religion of Jesus. At first Hegel accepts Kant's view that Jesus taught a pure morality, something like what Kant taught himself, a morality of duty derived from pure reason alone. In this state of mind Hegel writes a life of Jesus, working out Kant's views in detail. But he had too good an historical sense not to see that this was fantastic, and he begins to ask historical questions. What exactly was the message of Jesus, and to what was it opposed? It was opposed to Judaism as a religion which regarded God as purely objective and which consisted in serving him by obeying a series of statutory commands affecting every aspect of national and personal life, and in receiving support and subsistence in return. The teaching of Jesus was the very reverse of this. God is a loving father of his children; the divine is not a far-off object, but dwells also in the heart of man. The Kantian conception of duty enslaves the heart to the head. Love is the bond which should subsist between men, and the Kingdom of God is a community of loving hearts. Small communities of this kind there might be, but this bond of love could never unite a nation. Church and State could never become one. Christianity had seen a link between the divine and the human in Jesus, but when it united the divine with a specific historical individual, it failed to solve the problem of uniting infinite with finite, the problem which some years later (1822) Hegel was to describe as 'the most difficult, and yet the only, topic for philosophy'.[2]

[1] A reader unfamiliar with Hegel may find this chapter the most difficult in the book. I have done my best to make it intelligible, but Hegel's terminology has been found obscure even by many Germans, and it cannot be translated into English without much circumlocution, or without far longer explanation than the scale of this book allows. Some passages in this chapter which are repetitive have been left in the hope that they will shed light on one another.

[2] *Hegel Studien*, vol. i (Bonn, 1961), p. 28. For my own approach to this problem, see below in Chapter 10.

Hegel is rejecting the Christianity of the creeds. He clings to the religion of Jesus. Never throughout his life will he abandon religion. But henceforth he does abandon nearly everything *historical* in the creeds. He has come finally to the conclusion that whatever truth there is in Christianity does not depend on, and is quite indifferent to, those historical statements in the creeds, on which, for most Christians, their faith has been founded.

A negative answer to the historical problem, or a refusal to face it, has come alive again in our own day. This makes it all the more important for us to see how Hegel in his later years changed and developed his attitude to the Christian religion. We are asking: What can reason let us believe? Can we follow Hegel in the answer he provides? I shall try to answer this question at the end of this chapter.

So far we have dealt only with manuscripts which Hegel never published himself. His first publication which touches on our subject is his essay on *Faith and Knowledge*, published in 1802, three or four years after he had written *The Spirit of Christianity and its Fate*.

Hegel begins by maintaining that the distinction between faith and knowledge had taken a new form at the end of the eighteenth century. By arguing that there could be no knowledge of things in themselves, but only of phenomena, Kant had made room for faith, but only at the cost of making philosophy the handmaid of theology once more. Although, Kant holds, God can and must be *thought* by reason, he cannot be *known*, and therefore he is neither 'for' reason (as in the Middle Ages), nor 'against' reason (as in the Enlightenment's polemic against the positivity of religion and its miracles), but 'above' reason. Against this view Hegel argues that it does justice neither to faith nor to reason, neither to religion nor to philosophy. He claims for philosophy a *knowledge* of God, and urges that it is necessary to look beyond the 'positive' element in religion to the fundamental ideas which it contains. Faith and reason chime in together.

Most of the essay is an attack on what Hegel regards as the 'subjectivist' philosophies of Jacobi, Kant, and Fichte. But there are numerous allusions to Christian theology, and the way in which it is interpreted in them may be said to stand midway between *The Spirit of Christianity* and the later lectures on the philosophy of religion. Two examples of Hegel's philosophical theology may suffice:

First: If infinity is opposed to finitude, then the one is as finite as the other. . . . If the Absolute is supposed to be put together out of the finite and the infinite, then the removal of the finite would of course be a loss. But, in the Idea, infinite and finite are one, and, on this account, in so far as finitude as such had been supposed to have absolute truth and reality in itself, it has vanished. But it is only what was negative in it that has been negated, so that the true affirmation has been established.[1] These abstract phrases derive from a belief in the unity of the divine and the human: God and his children are one life.

Secondly, in an attempt to clarify the foregoing passage, I praphrase the final paragraphs of Hegel's essay (pp. 344–6) as follows:

The Crucifixion, which Hegel calls 'the infinite grief', was an historical event, but it has persisted as the feeling on which the Protestant religion rests, the feeling, as Luther said, that 'God is dead'. This negation is an essential moment or element in the being of God, for without it he is an abstract infinite, or indeed an abyss of nothingness in which all determinate being is lost. The Resurrection, however, negates the negation, and God is revealed as positively Spirit, the unity of infinite and finite. If God does not first negate his infinity, his infinity can never be concrete.

Now this must be translated into philosophy if philosophy is ever to grasp truth concretely as the Idea, i.e. the unity of concept and reality, form and content, subject and object, and if it is ever to be a philosophy of the infinite instead of the finite only. Philosophy must be given its 'speculative Good Friday' if it is to comprehend these opposites as a totality. That is to say that philosophy must submit to negation, to the 'power of the negative' which drives philosophy forward from the abstractions of logic, which, as lacking content, are infinite, to the finitude of nature, and then forward again to the true infinite, the unity of self-consciousness and the world, the unity of the Absolute Idea.

With this paraphrase compare the following passage from the essay on the *Scientific Methods of considering Natural Law*, which shows clearly how Hegel's interpretation of Christianity is intertwined with his metaphysics: 'The Absolute ever plays with itself a moral tragedy in which it ever gives birth to itself in the objective world, then in this form of itself gives itself over to suffering and death, and then raises itself out of its ashes to glory.'[2]

[1] *Erste Druckschriften*, ed. G. Lasson (Leipzig, 1928), pp. 232–4.
[2] *Werke*,[1] i, p. 386.

It is in this way that at this stage Hegel translates dogmatic theology into philosophy and so reconciles faith and reason.

In 1807 Hegel published what later he used to describe as his 'voyage of discovery',[1] namely *The Phenomenology of Spirit*. Although there is a good deal in the book about religion, most of it is merely a foretaste of his lectures on the philosophy of religion, and here I need call attention to three passages only.

(i) The Enlightenment accuses religious faith of basing its certainty on some individual historical testimonies which, as historical, would not guarantee that degree of certainty which newspapers provide us with nowadays about any event. Further, it urges that the assurance of faith rests on the preservation of these testimonies, first, on paper, secondly, on the skill and honesty of their transfer from one paper to another, and, finally, on the correct interpretation of the sense of dead letters. In fact, however, it does not occur to faith to link its assurance to testimonies and chances of this kind. In its assurance, it is a naïve relation to its absolute object, a pure knowledge thereof, which does not intrude letters, papers, copyists into its consciousness of the absolute Being. . . . This consciousness is Spirit itself, which testifies to itself both within the individual consciousness and through the universal presence in it of the faith of all men. If faith draws from history that mode of grounding, or at least confirming, its belief, of which the Enlightenment accuses it, and really supposes and acts as if all rested on that, then it has already allowed itself to be infected by Enlightenment, and its endeavours to ground or confirm itself in that way are just evidence that it has caught the infection.[2] (The voice is Hegel's but we might almost be hearing some modern theologians, as we shall see in due course.)

(ii) What the self-revealing spirit is in its actuality is not to be derived from, as it were, unwinding its rich life in the community and tracing it back to its original threads, it may be to the ideas of the original imperfect community or even to what the real Man said. . . . The basis of this tracing back is the instinct to get at the Concept; but it confuses the origin, as the immediate existence of the first appearance [in history], with the simplicity of the Concept. By thus impoverishing the life of Spirit, by removing the idea of the community, . . . there arises not the Concept but mere externality and individuality, the historical mode of an immediate

[1] Quoted from K. L. Michelet by H. Falkenheim in his notes to Kuno Fischer's *Hegel* (Heidelberg, 1911), ii, p. 1201.

[2] *Werke*[1] ii, p. 419.

appearance, and the spiritless memory of a supposed individual figure and its past history (pp. 574–5).

This is not easy to understand. 'Concept' is my translation of *Begriff*. Others prefer 'notion', but that is no easier in English. (I have attempted an elucidation of the term in my translation of Hegel's *Philosophy of Right* (Oxford, 1942), pp. viii–ix.) The point is that Hegel is dismissing history and interpreting Christianity in the light (or darkness) of his own terminology. Compare the end of *The Spirit of Christianity* where it is suggested that clinging to the historical Jesus blinded the Apostles and the Fathers to the truth.

(iii) The metaphorical thinking of the community is not conceptual thinking. It has the content (of the latter) without its necessity, and it brings into the realm of pure consciousness not the form of conceptual thinking but the natural relations of father and son. . . . It retreats from this its proper pure object [the Concept] and is related to it only externally: the Concept is revealed to it by a stranger, and in this thought of Spirit it does not recognize itself. . . . It misconceives itself, throws away the content as well as the form, and, what is the same thing, reduces the content to an historical picture and an heirloom of tradition (pp. 577–8). In other words, religion clings to metaphorical language, and Christianity to history. Philosophy has superseded both.

If at this stage we ask Hegel what it is reasonable to believe, we get an answer that would seem to be even more negative than Kant's. The unity of the divine and the human was revealed in Christianity, but Hegel has translated this into the language of his philosophy. The metaphorical thinking peculiar to religion is unnecessary for those who can understand the translation. The historicity of the New Testament seems to have ceased to interest Hegel. His attitude to that problem was probably that of an agnostic. These passages in the *Phenomenology* represent a more radically negative attitude to Christianity than he had either earlier or later.

The lectures on the *History of Philosophy*, which were prepared some years after the *Phenomenology* was published, contain one or two points which deserve special mention.

The leading idea in Christianity is the doctrine of the Trinity, which links infinite and finite, divine and human in the nature of God. This doctrine was worked out by the early Fathers. It is not to be found in the teaching of Jesus. It was only after his death that the Spirit was to come and guide men to the truth. It is therefore a great mistake to go back to the words of the New Testament and to try to find the essence of Christianity in the first beginnings of the teaching of the Apostles. The great merit of the Fathers is that, against heresies denying either the humanity or the divinity of Jesus, they held fast to the union of both natures. The Greek gods were not anthropomorphic enough: they dwelt apart on Olympus, and man was not divine as man.

Whereas, in *The Spirit of Christianity*, Hegel had disparaged the humanity of Jesus as something always dragging him down to earth, he now realizes that the humanity is essential. The Logos is made flesh. It is not enough to know that God is Spirit, or that the finite is a moment in his nature: that moment must appear, and so unite God with man. The Son of God is a real man, Christ. Nevertheless, the spiritual nature of man, his likeness to the divine, could not come home to men's hearts until after Jesus had died. Not in association with Jesus, or by attention to his words and life on earth, could men come to realize his divinity. The Dalai Lama is a real man, but Christianity brings God into men's hearts, and therefore Jesus could not remain present on earth. He sits on the right hand of God, as the Son and the Logos. This is what Spirit revealed after Jesus had died.[1]

Hegel had discovered in Christian doctrine the key to his whole philosophy. Man is Spirit, not nature. He must deny nature, or what he actually is, in order to become what he is implicitly, Spirit. His advance in spiritual life is by the negation or alienation of past achievement. The 'power of the negative', as Hegel was to say in his *Science of Logic*[2] is the spur to advance. But it is not something which supervenes from without. Spirit, as universal, negates itself in order to reach pure self-consciousness, but then it incorporates its negative within itelf, and so only is Spirit fully actual as unity of universal and particular, finite and infinite. Some may say that Hegel's synthesis of opposites is untenable philosophically, and that his interpretation of the Trinity is unacceptable theologically. But there can be no doubt that the religion came first, and that the philosophy had religion at its heart.

It was in these lectures that Hegel made his famous remark: I am and will remain a Lutheran.[3] But what did he mean? Here is his answer.

[1] *Werke*[1] xv, pp. 101–13.
[2] *ibid.*[1] iii, pp. 43 ff.
[3] *ibid.*[1] xiii, p. 89.

The Jewish religion was given to the Jews by Moses and the Prophets; it came to them from without. But this external transmission, no matter from what individual, is something historical, not affecting the religion's real content. The individual is not the content of the doctrine he teaches. But the peculiarity of the Christian religion is that the person, Christ, and his characteristic as Son of God, belongs to the nature of God himself. If Christ for the Christians were only a teacher, like Socrates, then this would be no revelation, no teaching about the nature of God, and it is this alone that we want to be taught. The historical content of Christianity, the life of Jesus, must become something *spiritual* for Spirit; it must cease to be external as historical facts are external. The ground of Christian faith is the testimony of Spirit to what it contains. The divine Spirit which is comprehended is objective: subjective Spirit comprehends. But Spirit is not passive but active, so that there is one spiritual substantial unity. 'This comprehension is what has been called faith. It is the faith of Lutherans, and it is not an historical faith.' How far Hegel's theological colleagues would have accepted this account of Lutheranism, I cannot say.

Whether orthodox or not, however, Hegel was certainly a deeply religious man. Those who have contested this have not studied his lectures on the *Philosophy of Religion* in the edition edited by G. Lasson.[1] Here we can read what Hegel wrote himself for his lectures, as well as what his pupils reported. In what follows I have confined myself in the main to what is authentically Hegel's.

Christianity begins by finding man at variance with himself; by nature he is not what he ought to be. By renouncing nature, however, he becomes conscious of himself as Spirit, and this is a revelation of God which reconciles man to himself and to God. Religion gives him a knowledge of God. It is not a matter of feeling alone; feeling is there, but in Christianity it is united with knowledge.

This is not realized by theologians (Hegel is thinking of his colleague—and opponent—Schleiermacher) who make the mistake of reducing religion to intuition or feeling, or who tend to do so, or else of forgetting feeling and emphasizing knowledge. But in the latter event what they are concerned with is not the knowledge of God, but with pedantry. They make a great fuss about historical

[1] *Leipzig*, 1925–30.

circumstances, biblical criticism, Church history, doctrinal decisions of Councils, and so forth. This is having to do with conceptions that others have had and fought about, with histories that we have no inkling of. Just as a blind man can feel the frame and the canvas of a picture but cannot see it, so these theologians with their historical preoccupations cannot grasp the real content and spirit of Christianity.

Those who cling to Scripture are just as bad. Every interpreter of the text brings with him his own presuppositions. Consequently the most diverse interpretations are available; theologians have made the Bible into a nose of wax, and all the heretics call upon Scripture just as much as the orthodox do.

Modern theologians [i.e. in the early nineteenth century] are likewarm about some fundamental Christian doctrines, like the Trinity, for example. This is an instance of philosophy's upholding a doctrine better than theologians do. They are inclined to follow Kant and say that reason can know nothing of God, and thus they reduce the name of God to an empty word, the object of feeling, maybe, but not knowledge. God, however, is Spirit, no empty word; but, if so, then God must be three in one, for that is the nature of Spirit. God makes himself an object to himself, i.e. in the son; he remains in this object, but then, in this differentiation of himself from himself, he at the same time annuls the difference and in it loves himself, i.e. is identical with himself, comes together with himself in this love of his own. Thus only is God Spirit; only the Trinity is the nature of God as Spirit.

In this way philosophy justifies this basic Christian doctrine. Theologians do research on Greek philosophy and Neo-Platonism to find out where it came from, but these historical inquiries are valueless. What is ignored is the witness of Spirit to Spirit. The historians are like bank clerks, entering the money transactions of others with nothing of their own.

As Plato said, we do not learn so much as remember, or discover by reflection what is within. Religion may be taught to us in youth, but in fact it can never be imposed on anyone. It can only be aroused in us. We are implicitly Spirit; this is what we are meant to be; to bring this into consciousness is to believe, to know a spiritual unity with the absolute Spirit.

It is useless to rely on feeling, especially a feeling of dependence —animals have that. If Schleiermacher were right, then 'a dog would be the best Christian'.[1] Only man has religion. Feeling of course is necessary, but only as accompanying knowledge, never its foundation. I cannot feel God, but, knowing him, I can feel grateful to him.

Religious language, to be sure, is metaphorical. When we speak of God engendering a son, we know that this is metaphor or myth. The same is true of the tree of the knowledge of good and evil. It is silly to ask what tree this was. Even the story of Jesus is not simply to be taken literally. It is not simply an ordinary story of a man. The story has the divine as its content, and this is the inner substantial truth with which reason is concerned. This is always Hegel's mature view of history as a whole. Historians may recount a series of events, but reason descries their inner truth, and that alone is what matters.

Hegel draws a careful distinction between art and religion. Art is pictorial; religion, however, has not pictures but *Vorstellungen*, which I think is best translated in this context by 'metaphors', because Hegel insists that, unlike pictures, they are thoughts. The task of philosophy is to change into conceptual form what in religion has a metaphorical form. The content of religion is identical with the content of philosophy, i.e. truth. It may be suggested that, by its work of translation, philosophy is becoming a substitute for religion, or making religion unnecessary, but this is not so. Philosophy has to do with nothing *less* than to upset religion, as if the content of religion were not itself the truth. Indeed, religion *is* truth, but in the form of metaphor; substantial truth has not been given first by philosophy. Men did not have to wait for philosophy before they could come to knowledge of the truth. The philosophy in question here is what Hegel calls 'speculative' philosophy, i.e. his own.

It is when theologians cling to the form in which their religious doctrines are couched that they become vulnerable to attack from the philosophy of what is called the 'Enlightenment' (though it should rather be called the 'eclipse')[2] with its *raisonnement* (always a pejorative word in Hegel) which will make short work of them. Religion puts into space and time what philosophy sees *sub specie aeternitatis*, an essential moment in the life of God.

Luther was right to insist on justification by faith, but only if faith is not merely knowing the catechism, but is accepted, not

[1] *Werke*[1] xvii, p. 295.

[2] *ibid.* xi, p. 34.

from without or on authority, but on the testimony of my own inner spirit.

The finite has its being not in itself but in an Other, and this Other is the infinite. Man, conscious of finitude, lifts himself to the infinite, and this is religion, a consciousness that the finite has its real being in the infinite. In Christianity this is a real union of spirits. To say that God is outside and above us is like threshing empty straw. God, the absolute Spirit, must have the character of finitude within himself. This may seem blasphemous, but if the finite is not within the infinite, but outside and alongside it, the infinite is degraded to being just another finite. When the finite is opposed to God, it is taken to be something self-subsistent on its own account, whereas it is nothing of the kind. This may be regarded as a contradiction, and so it is and remains for abstract thinking. But every living thing, everything concrete and actual is a contradiction: man, for example, both is and is not Spirit.

What Jesus taught was not Christian dogmatics, the doctrine of the Church. He taught the Kingdom of God. This was a revolutionary doctrine, because it involved the complete negation of the whole existing order. Nowhere is preaching so revolutionary as it is in the Gospels, because everything that is valid otherwise is set down there as a matter of indifference, deserving no attention.[1] Jesus will not allow a man who wanted to follow him to go home first and take leave of his relations. He asks: Who is my mother? Who are my brethren? Thus he breaks all moral ties. Property ties fare no better. Care nothing for the morrow. Give your goods to the poor. This was teaching which had to be abandoned when the Kingdom of God did not come.

The death of Jesus is not to be understood as just the death of this individual. The point is that 'God is dead'. This absolute grief, this negation of spirit, is negatived in turn by the Resurrection, by God's return into himself. Before his death, Jesus is one man amongst others, a teacher and a friend. It is his death that makes him a revelation of God. The gift of the Spirit after his death made the Apostles realize this. They had the Spirit to lead them into all truth. They did not need miracles. It is of no interest to discuss what was drunk at Cana. No doubt they began by thinking of the individual, but the factual appearance of the man was transformed into the recogniton of him as Son of God. Even today a start may be made with the empirical, with the

[1] *Phil. d. Geschichte*, ed. G. Lasson (Leipzig, 1920), p. 740.

Gospel record, miracles, and the like. But this is only a beginning: it has to be negated, because it is all past, whereas Spirit is present and active, and the way of faith is by Spirit alone. The content of faith is to be justified by philosophy, not by history, which is always open to doubt. To go to Scripture and treat it as a collection of books like those written by profane authors is all very well if you are dealing with history and finitude, instead of with the eternal and absolute truth. Scripture must be interpreted spiritually and not philologically.

By this time Hegel's development and final position should be clear enough, whatever difficulties there are in it in principle or in detail. But there are some points of interest in his lectures on the *Proofs of the Existence of God* which he was preparing for publication when he died. They are important for our consideration of what it is reasonable to believe.

'Faith' is reserved for Christianity. The Greeks had no 'faith' in Zeus. A clash between faith and reason would be the most agonizing diremption in the depth of our spirit. But there should be no clash. How could God contradict himself by making man in thinking, the essence of his Spirit, contradict what has come to him by communication from on high? Anselm was right to say that it would be negligence, once we are confirmed in *faith*, not to seek to *understand* what we believe.[1]

It is useless to say that we know that God exists but that we know nothing about him, or that we have a relation to him and he none to us. A one-sided relation is no relation at all. God is not envious or jealous. He reveals himself. It is the nature of Spirit to remain in possession of its own, while it puts another in possession of it. God does not reveal himself to plants or animals, but only to man. Spirit reveals itself to Spirit alone, and the essence of man's Spirit is thinking. It is not the so-called 'limited' reason of man that knows God, but the Spirit of God in man; God's self-knowing knows itself in man's knowing.

Spirit lifts itself to God. What is of the greatest importance is to be clear about this connection of infinite with finite. This topic is the deepest, the most sublime, and therefore the most difficult.

As long ago as 1795 Hegel wrote to Schelling that he had once intended to try to make clear to himself in an essay what it means

[1] This quotation from *Cur Deus Homo?* is a favourite of Hegel's. When it is read in its context one may wonder whether his use of it is fair.

to draw near to God. This is the problem which now, in 1831, he thinks he has solved. It cannot be solved by using finite categories, i.e. those that we use for the description of ordinary life or in empirical science. The union of God and man is a union of Spirit with Spirit. The difficulty is to hold fast to the difference of the two and yet preserve the union. The Spirit of man whereby he knows God is just the Spirit of God himself. Here Hegel is adapting for his own purpose words which elsewhere he quotes from Eckhart: 'The eye with which God sees me is the eye with which I see him; my eye and his eye are one.'[1]

Before attempting to assess the worth of Hegel's writings on religion, I conclude the process of summary and quotation by drawing attention to one or two passages in the *Philosophy of History*.

History is the execution of the plan of God's providence. To descry this plan is thought to be presumptuousness by those who say that God cannot be known. But true humility consists in knowing God in everything, honouring him in everything, especially in history. If God could not be known, then nothing could interest the human spirit except the godless, the restricted, the finite. To be sure, we must make our account with the finite; but the higher necessity is that we should have a Sunday on which to lift ourselves above the affairs of week-days, make our account with truth, and bring this into consciousness.[2]

We are wrong to remember Christ as just an historical person who lived in the past. If he is regarded as an excellent and even sinless man, and no more, then the portrayal of the speculative Idea, absolute truth, is falsified. But it is with the latter that we have to do and to begin. Belief in the divinity of Christ is the witness of one's own Spirit, not the witness of miracles, for only Spirit knows Spirit. The mystery of the Christian religion is this link between the divine and the human, the discovery that a man has infinite worth in himself because he is the recipient of divine grace. Show as you like that orthodox doctrines have been settled by this or that interest or passion of the bishops; make what you like of Christ exegetically, critically, historically, all these things may be what they like; the only question is what the Idea or truth is in and for itself.[3]

[1] *Phil. d. Rel.*, ed. G. Lasson, Part i (Leipzig, 1925), p. 257.
[2] *Phil. d. Geschichte*, ed. G. Lasson (Leipzig, 1917), pp. 18–19.
[3] *ibid.*, pp. 737–8.

Having now exhibited Hegel's views at a length which some will regard as inordinate, I must attempt an assessment. If it seems negative, perhaps the positive side will come before us later. The space devoted to Hegel is justified, in my view, partly because his influence was immense in the nineteenth century, and partly because the development of his ideas is of great interest to those who survey the contemporary scene and think of theological history over the last, say, eighty years.

Kant, as we have seen, regarded religion as a prop for morality, a prop which would gradually become less and less necessary as mankind learnt to derive morality from pure reason alone, and to interpret philosophically or morally the doctrines of Christian orthodoxy. Jesus, Kant thought, had taught a pure morality, but this came to be misrepresented, and the whole paraphernalia of orthodoxy took its place. Hegel started by accepting most of this, but he attached more importance to religion as part and parcel of national and personal life than Kant did.

Although Hegel accepted from Lessing the view that religious faith cannot rest on historical facts, and although this was a view from which he never swerved in his later years, he had a much greater historical sense than Kant had, and he soon saw that, whatever Jesus taught, it was not the pure morality of Kant. Love was Christ's watchword, not law, whether the positive law of Judaism, or the moral law of Kant's pure reason. Christianity, however, is not to be found in what Jesus taught. Only after his death did the Spirit reveal to the Disciples the unity of divine and human in Jesus, and so pave the way for the elaboration of the doctrine of the Trinity by the early Fathers.

This faith grasps the truth. The happiness of Greek religion is like the innocence of childhood, something which has to be lost if man is to enter into a spiritual life. Negation, grief, is the price of progress. The Cross was necessary if man was to be made conscious of Spirit, of the unity of divine and human, if he was to be reconciled, once he had become conscious of the fact that he was not what he ought to be. It is one thing to grasp the truth by faith, but man's essence as Spirit is his thinking. Faith does include thinking within itself; it is not mere feeling; but it must become an object of thought so that the thinking in it may be made explicit. Philosophy must strip off the form in which the faith is expressed in order to reveal its content. The language of religion turns out to be metaphorical or mythical; philosophy translates it.

This is to make explicit a distinction between symbol and meaning which religion never makes explicit. For example, it might be held that the Incarnation symbolized the identity of spirit and matter, the Atonement the fact that the way to goodness lies through evil, the Holy Spirit the union of infinite and finite.

In one of his earliest manuscripts Hegel remarks: 'Love is somewhat analogous to reason. Love finds itself in others, or, rather, forgetting itself, places itself outside its own being, lives as it were in others, feels and is active in them, while reason, as the general principle of valid laws, knows itself again in every rational being as a fellow-citizen of an intelligible world.'[1] In the *Philosophy of Religion* he writes: 'It is true to say that God is love, but consider what love is. It is a distinguishing of two people who nevertheless are for one another not distinguished. The consciousness or feeling of this identity, and this being outside oneself and in another is love. . . . God is love, this distinguishing and the negation of this distinction.'[2]

Hegel had early wrestled with the problem of opposites, finite and infinite, subject and object. He found his answer in meditating on the nature of love, the centre of the teaching of Jesus, and on the discourses in St John's Gospel (I and my Father are one, etc.). If the opposites are simply taken as contradicting one another, and as it were on the same level with one another, no union of them is possible. But Hegel's meditations on love provided him with a clue. As he said, 'what is a contradiction in the realm of the dead is not one in the realm of life'.[3] Life is process, and the process advances by negation. He who loses his life shall find it. This is the process of thinking. A universal is abstract until it is negatived in the particular, but the concrete, a unity of universal and particular, is reached by the negation of the particular, whereby the universal returns into itself. This is the continual process of mind, *Geist*, spirit. And this is the process of spirit in its infinity: it carries the negation within itself; it particularizes itself, and yet overcomes the contradiction by remaining at one with itself.

In this way, beginning with a religion of love, Hegel arrives at his *Logic* and at a translation of the metaphors of religion into the categories of philosophy. Does this make religion superfluous? Certainly not for those who are not philosophers. But what about

[1] Nohl, *op. cit.*, p. 18.
[2] *Phil. d. Religion*, ed. G. Lasson, iii, pt. 1, p. 75.
[3] *Early Theological Writings*, Eng. tr., p. 261.

the philosophers? Hegel insists that philosophy is not a substitute for religion; its content is the same. But can this be accepted? If religion declares something to be a fact, or founded on fact, or a truth, and philosophy shows that it is only a symbol (or metaphor) which philosophy has translated, how can the symbol have any further value? A material object may serve as a symbol, and we may still retain it and value it when we know what it means. But a doctrine or an alleged historical fact is something different. The doctrine can remain of value only to those who do not know, or who cannot translate, its symbolic character. And if the alleged historical fact is only a symbol, it ceases to be a fact, and can no longer be alleged as such.

By holding that historical inquiry is irrelevant to the Christian faith, and then that what remains of that faith can be translated from metaphor into philosophy, Hegel would seem to suggest that Christians, even the most intelligent of them, are believing lies. The saints have lived and acted accepting myth or metaphor as fact, and could not have lived and acted as they did if they had not had that faith. This suggests that Hegel's view of religion, and especially of Christianity, is inadequate. Theologians may well say of his philosophical defence of orthodoxy: *Non tali auxilio.*

There is something to be said on the other side. Hegel himself could not give up religion. It is almost as if he were unconvinced by his own arguments. He remarks: 'Just as the man said to his wife when she complained about the weather, "it's better than no weather at all", so it is better to have a poor religion than none.'[1] Moreover, Hegel never says that God is a metaphor, even if Father and Son are figurative expressions. And what is most significant of all is Hegel's use of the word *Geist*. It means 'mind', but it also means 'spirit', and on *Geist*, as the supreme Idea, his whole philosophy is built. As I have shown, he learnt his philosophy from his study of religion. Is his philosophy not itself religious, based as it is on *Geist*? Is his philosophy not simply a religion, a sort of drastic Christian modernism? If faith can be understood by translation into philosophy, is faith not thereby destroyed? Our answer might well be that a good deal of faith is needed for the acceptance of Hegel's philosophy, which is not intelligible without its religious basis. On the other hand, his philosophy of religion would seem to dissolve history into philosophy, and so to leave no place for the uniqueness of Jesus.

[1] *Proofs of the Existence of God, Werke*[1], xii, p. 402.

However that may be, the greatest defect in Hegel's later writings on religion is his refusal to see that for Christianity the vital questions are those raised by history and biblical criticism. These were raised in part by Reimarus and Lessing and Hegel himself tackled historical questions in his earlier writings. Most of his essay on *The Spirit of Christianity* still holds good. It is biblical criticism, however, which now comes to the fore, and it is this, combined with history, that we now have to face.

CHAPTER 7

STRAUSS AND MODERNISM

The influence of Hegel on intellectual life in Germany, certainly in the nineteenth century, if not later, cannot be exaggerated. The domination of his philosophy was short-lived; but it was his teaching which led to scholarly work in the editing of classical texts, and to the philological and historical scrutiny of the Bible. Here Germany was the spearhead of scholarship. In history too Germany was a leader, but this new interest in history, and a new understanding of past epochs, was inspired from more than one source. One was Scott's novels, and this was common to most countries in western Europe. Hegel's philosophy of religion, with its neglect of history, has received a new lease of life in this century from those known as Form-Critics.

German work on the Bible was late in influencing these islands. In the first four decades of the nineteenth century, hardly anyone in the English universities could read German. In 1824 there were in Oxford only two.[1] Pusey, then a young man of twenty-four, who had just graduated, accepted a suggestion from the Professor of Divinity that he 'should learn something about these German critics'. He learnt German, spent a long period in Germany at various universities, and met most of the leading theologians. The fruit of his studies was published in 1828 in his *Historical Enquiry into the Probable Causes of the Rationalist Character of the Theology of Germany*. The chief cause he identified as 'orthodoxism', a word which he adopted from Lessing, and which was meant to mean a 'dead orthodoxy'. This word was misunderstood as implying that Pusey himself was unorthodox, an implication strengthened by his asserting that historical passages in the Bible, in which no religious truth was contained, were not equally inspired with the rest. This misunderstanding he constantly repudiated, but he feared that his book had done harm; it was withdrawn and he ordered that it be not republished. Although he had no sympathy with the more extreme rationalists, he took an optimistic view of German theology's future. He describes the rationalist theology as '*lately* predominant',[2] and believed that religion would gain permanently from its rude contact with rationalism. How

[1] H. P. Liddon: *Life of Pusey* (London, 1894), i, p. 72.
[2] *ibid.*, pp. 146 ff. My italics.

mistaken he was became clear in 1835 when D. F. Strauss published his *Life of Jesus*.

George Eliot's translation of this work (i.e. of its fourth edition, 1840) did not appear until 1846. Meantime the ecclesiastical scene in both England and Scotland was dominated by controversies untouched by biblical criticism or rationalist theology. The Oxford Movement and the Disruption both started from a reconsideration of the relation between the established Church and the State. In both cases the rebels, or innovators, believed in an established Church, but they were demanding freedom in purely ecclesiastical matters. In Scotland there was no doctrinal difference between the Free Kirk and the Auld, but in England the Tractarians, harking back to the seventeenth-century divines, were reasserting a high doctrine of the Church which was not always palatable to the Evangelicals in their own Communion.

All parties accepted as an article of faith the plenary inspiration of the Bible, and disputes arose only about certain dogmas, as, for example, baptismal regeneration expounded heretically by Mr Gorham, or the Atonement expounded heretically by Mr McLeod Campbell.

The Tractarians appealed to the Vincentian Canon: The faith was what had been believed always, everywhere, by everyone. While Vincent seems to have interpreted this without rigidity,[1] it is at least an appeal to antiquity, to the period before the Great Schism, and it effectively precludes acceptance of nineteenth-century biblical criticism, and it also sets aside the historical problems which seem to me to be vital. In 1845 Pusey wrote: 'If we throw ourselves in entire faith upon the early undivided church and say dogmatically. . . . "This is the truth, the voice of the whole church" . . . this will tell.'[2] He was convinced that it was necessary to have a strong, positive, objective system which people are to believe, because it is true, on an authority other than their own selves (*ibid.*). This attitude reminds me of the advisers of King Canute. Strauss had published his epoch-making book ten years earlier. Pusey's reaction to it was expressed in a letter to Newman in 1839: 'It is very shocking that Strauss's book should be doing harm in Cambridge or that . . . they should even be reading it. I know nothing, except from general report, about it; so I cannot imagine that any there should not be offended with it as a

[1] N. P. Williams, in *Northern Catholicism* (London, 1933), pp. 185 ff.
[2] *Life*, edn. cit., ii, 489.

whole, such as it is described.'[1] Obscurantism could hardly go further.

George Eliot's translation of Strauss's *Life* was reissued with an introduction by Pfleiderer in 1892 and was later reprinted once or twice. It has long been out of print and my efforts to buy a copy have failed. Thus, although everyone has heard of the book, and many suppose it to be a monument of infidelity, long ago discredited, few today seem to have read it, and it may be worth while to devote some space to its examination.

Perhaps I should say at once that, although George Eliot 'was thoroughly bored with it, and only her strong sense of duty made her complete'[2] her translation, it is one of the most brilliant and one of the most fascinating books that I have ever read.

Like Reimarus, for whom he had a great admiration, Strauss was a master of style. His meaning is never in doubt. The book is about half a million words long, but none of them is wasted. It is scholarly and extraordinarily learned, but the learning is carried lightly. Strauss has a gift for epigram and an agreeable sarcasm. When he headed one of his chapters: 'Sea stories and fish stories', he was taken to task by his critics for flippancy. But it is much easier to say, with Pusey, 'offensive', or, with others, 'flippant', than to answer Strauss's arguments. No book that I know has ever been better argued. He can be ignored; he can be accused of infidelity; but all this is not to the purpose. His argument must be met by argument. What is called the 'climate of opinion' today is a climate in which Strauss did not live, but he deserves to be met face to face on his own terms. This can be done. It would perhaps not have surprised him if the study of the New Testament had made some advance since his day. But I suspect that Strauss has not so much been refuted as left unread. I shall argue that there are points at which we must part company with Strauss, but he has made to our historical problem a contribution which is secure.

Strauss was born in 1808. He was a pupil of F. C. Baur at Tübingen. He was only twenty-seven when his masterpiece was published. Seldom has a man so young produced a book so learned, so wide-ranging, so profound. Schweitzer's *Quest of the Historical Jesus* is the nearest parallel that I can recollect. The book wrecked Strauss's career, but 'it marked an epoch in the history of theology'.[3]

[1] *Life*, edn. cit., ii, p. 109.
[2] H. G. Wood: *Belief and Unbelief since* 1850 (Cambridge, 1955), p. 122.
[3] O. Pfleiderer, in his Preface to the 1892 edition of George Eliot's translation.

When Strauss was a student, German theologians who wrote on the New Testament were divided into two camps. First, there were traditionalists, like Olshausen, who accepted miracles and everything supernatural in the New Testament, and, secondly, rationalists, like Paulus, Hegel's friend, who accepted the narratives as historical, but explained away their miraculous element. Strauss was dissatisfied with both. He agreed with the rationalists in rejecting the miraculous, but disagreed with their attempts to rationalize the New Testament record. What we are confronted with, Strauss argues, when we encounter the miraculous in the New Testament is not a fact at all, not a fact to be accepted as miracle or explained as natural, but a myth. By a 'myth' we are not to understand a 'fairy-tale', but rather a pictorial or metaphorical representation of a truth which can be apprehended by most people only in this mythical form. (The influence of Hegel is fairly obvious.) Thus Strauss can say: 'The essence of the Christian faith is perfectly independent of my criticism. The supernatural birth of Christ, his miracles, his Resurrection and Ascension, remain eternal truths, whatever doubts may be cast on their reality as historical facts'. One wonders whether Bultmann, for example, ever fell under the spell of Strauss.

Strauss objected to Kant's forced interpretation of the Scriptures that Kant had failed to show the relation between the words of Scripture and the moral ideas which he derived thereform, and of which the biblical words were symbolical representations; nor did Kant make any attempt to show how it happened that the one came to be expressed by the other (pp. 51–2).[1] A similar criticism has been urged against Strauss: How came it about that the philosophical ideas with which his book ends were expressed, apparently in the language of history, but actually, according to Strauss, in the form of myth? He does, however, supply an answer to this question. Myths, he believes, with examples before him from cultures other than the Hebraic, are the necessary vehicle of expression for the first efforts of the human mind (p. 53). The Hebrews did not distinguish between history and fiction so clearly as we do. The mythical element in the New Testament was the product, not of any intention to deceive, but of accepting the traditional characteristics of the Messiah, together with the belief that Jesus was the Messiah, such was the overwhelming impression

[1] All my page references to Strauss's book are to the 1898 edition of George Eliot's translation.

made on his contemporaries by his personal character, discourses, and miracles of healing (p. 85). This is a reasonable reply, but when Strauss proceeds to derive philosophical ideas from what is left after his critical work, he fails, just as Kant did, to show the connection between these ideas and the New Testament narratives; nor can he explain how, if these ideas were ever held before Hegel's time, they came to be expressed in historical or mythical form. His explanation of how the myths in the New Testament arose itself precludes an answer to this troublesome question. The same problem, without any solution, seems to me to have confronted Bultmann a century and more later.

It is important to realize that Strauss was just as much opposed to the rationalists, whose recent predominance in Germany Pusey so deeply deplored, as to supernaturalists like Pusey himself. The sort of rationalism which he was opposing may become clear from the following examples:

(i) Reimarus had objected to the story of the Fall that it made God issue an arbitrary command, not to eat the fruit of the tree. The rationalist Eichhorn replies: Who knows that the command was arbitrary or capricious? The tree was very likely a poisonous one, the fruit of which would harm a man. Perhaps Adam saw an animal die in convulsions after eating the fruit, but then later saw a snake eat the fruit without coming to any harm. Then, despite the warning, Adam ran the risk of eating, which brought death to him, not at once, but later, and this had moral and physical consequences for his descendants!

(ii) When Jesus was taken from the cross and laid in the tomb, he was thought to be dead, but he really was not; later he came to. His reappearance startled the Disciples, who, despite all his efforts to prove the contrary, insisted on treating him as a supernatural being![1] With such flights of imagination Strauss had no sympathy.

Strauss's method is to set forth the New Testament narrative or narratives of an event; to point out contradictions, if any, and there are plenty, between the narratives; to expound the solutions for difficulties, arising in the narratives or from their contradictions, which had been propounded by theologians, both supernaturalist and rationalist; and to discuss the adequacy, or more commonly the inadequacy, of these solutions. This method is pursued

[1] Quoted from Strauss: *Der alte und der neue Glaube* (Leipzig, 1872), pp. 38–40.

thoroughly and relentlessly, and with extraordinary ingenuity and scholarship, from the Annunciation of John the Baptist to the Ascension of Jesus. Strauss remarks that this method has the extrinsic advantage that his book provides a repertory of the principal opinions and treatises concerning all parts of the evangelical history. The opinions from which Strauss dissents are fairly stated, and a reader may accept them and reject Strauss if he thinks fit.

It is impossible to convey the flavour of Strauss, his scholarship, his ingenuity, his clarity, his incisiveness, his thoroughness, without quoting pages of his work *in extenso*. However, in order to give an example of his procedure, I summarize very briefly his treatment of the Temptation in the wilderness.

A complete fast for forty days is incredible. The personal appearance of the devil is inconceivable. The words used in the Gospels imply that the devil transported Jesus from place to place magically. Expositors (some of them orthodox) who suppose that the change of place was effected naturally, in that Jesus set out on a journey and the devil followed him, suppose something which is not in the Scriptures and is directly contradictory to what is there. If we ask where the mountain is, from the summit of which all the kingdoms of the world can be seen, the answer that 'world' here means only Palestine is almost as ludicrous as the other suggestion that the devil pointed out all the kingdoms of the world on a map.

Attempts to answer these difficulties by supposing that the whole thing was a dream are quite unconvincing, and they have no warrant in the text. Consequently the entire episode is regarded as real but natural; the tempter was an artful Pharisee; the angels who ministered to Jesus's hunger were either a caravan with provisions or soft reviving breezes. Strauss refuses to waste words on refuting this nonsense.

The Temptation in the wilderness, Strauss argues, cannot have taken place in the manner described in the Gospels. It is a Christian myth or legend put together out of Old Testament material. What makes this view so convincing depends on the wealth of detail in Strauss's argument from the Old Testament, and no mere summary can do it justice.

Strauss points out that, if Jesus was a man like ourselves, really a man, despite what Docetism may say, then he cannot have had power to raise the dead, to walk on the sea, or to still a storm.

His treatment of the Transfiguration is of interest. He regards it as a myth drawn from passages in the Old Testament. (I myself have seen three shafts of light piercing a rain cloud on a hill, but, tempted to see there the origin of the Transfiguration, I have Strauss against me, for then I am being a rationalist, and he would ask me how I explain the rest of the narrative. And his mythical explanation is one which there may be no rational ground for rejecting.)

For Strauss a natural explanation of the Transfiguration reduces it to triviality. If the splendour around Jesus was only an optical phenomenon, and if the two appearances with him were either dream images or unknown men, where is the significance of the event? If instead it is seen to be a myth, then its importance can be understood: it exhibits in the life of Jesus an enhanced repetition of the glorification of Moses; and, by the appearance of the Lawgiver and the Prophet, Jesus is represented as the perfecter of the Kingdom of God, the fulfilment of the Law and the Prophets and there is confirmation of his messianic dignity by a heavenly voice (pp. 545–6).

If Strauss explains as myth everything supernatural in the New Testament, we may reasonably ask whether anything historical remains. But we do not get any very clear answer. Strauss certainly regarded Jesus as an historical character who believed himself to be the Messiah, and was accepted as such by many. The discourses in the Synoptics contain the teaching of Jesus like morsels of granite which could not be dissolved by oral tradition; but they have often been polished and misplaced. The Lord's Prayer is made up of Jewish formulae, but the selection and arrangement of them is entirely original and bears the impress of the religious consciousness which Jesus possessed and which he tried to impart to his followers. It also seems certain that the eschatological passages are authentic. Strauss's strongest expression about this is as follows: 'Either we can found nothing historical on the Gospels, or else Jesus expected to appear on the clouds of heaven in the immediate future at the start of the Messianic kingdom which he had proclaimed.'[1] Nor can it be doubted that Jesus was crucified and that afterwards the Disciples believed in his Resurrection. But 'I can only indicate how uncertain everything about the life of Jesus is; how little we can be sure even in the

[1] *Der alte und der neue Glaube*, edn cit., p. 80. Professor Black has told me that although Paul took literally the saying recorded in Mark xiv. 62, this may not have been what Jesus meant.

speeches and teaching of Jesus whether the words and thoughts are his or only such as were put into his mouth by others later' (*ibid.*, p. 58). 'The Jesus of history is a problem; but a problem is not an object of faith' (*ibid.*, p. 79). Strauss's scepticism increased with the years, perhaps because he realized that there was no room for faith in his philosophical dogmatics.

Nevertheless, what seems to be lacking is a clear appreciation of the uniqueness of Jesus without which Christianity could never have come into being. When at the end of his book Strauss 'restores dogmatically' what he had 'destroyed critically', Jesus has no more relation to the Christian myths than other human beings have. Like Hegel, Strauss at the end has rather evaded the historical problem than faced it.

This is not the only shortcoming in his book. For example, he is apt to use as a standard his own limpid style and scholarly lack of repetition. Thus we cannot follow him when he claims that the same words cannot have been spoken of Jesus on different occasions.[1] Nor can we accept his scepticism when he shows that, in comparing the Synoptics, we find contradictions about the time and place of an event, which must be admitted, and then infers that the event is not historical but mythical.[2] Lessing was right, in reply to Reimarus, to emphasize that many differences between the Evangelists in details are insufficient to disprove the reality of the event which they are describing.

Moreover, Strauss's work is dated. Although he was himself doubtful about the ascription of the first and fourth Gospels to Disciples who were eye-witnesses, he does often argue that his contemporary theologians were right to give primacy to Matthew and John; and yet he shows that John cannot be accepted as historical.[3] He regards Mark as an imitator of Matthew. Thus, like the early Reimarus, he took the Gospel records as more or less on one footing; he did not examine them critically. His negative criticism, however, led to this examination, and it in turn destroyed some of Strauss's arguments which had been based on the findings of the precritical era.

I have given reasons for departing from some things in Strauss's great book. But one thing I think he has done, and done conclusively for anyone who has not got to submit to authority. He has completely demolished the supposed inerrancy of the Bible. However many of the contradictions in Scripture to which he draws

[1] *Life*, p. 397 *et al.* [2] *ibid.*, p. 350 *et al.* [3] *ibid.*, p. 509.

attention are contradictions in what Lessing called *Kleinigkeiten*, trivialities, others affect matters of substance, and no student of Strauss will forget or deny them. I need only cite Strauss's searching analysis of the genealogies in Matthew and Luke. They are at variance with one another, and if both are meant to prove a Davidic descent, they disprove the Virgin Birth.

Reimarus wrote over two centuries ago, Strauss over one century ago. But these two men, little read nowadays even by scholars and theologians (if I may judge from their writings), still present a challenge to those who ask themselves what they may reasonably believe, and who therefore vex themselves with the problem of Christian origins and the historicity of the New Testament.

Since Strauss proceeded all through his book on the assumption that miracles did not happen, and that the miraculous events recorded in the New Testament did not happen, this may be a suitable point at which to touch upon the question of miracle. A miracle is supposed to be a divine intervention in the course of nature, wrought either directly by God or indirectly through someone on whom God has conferred the power to work miracles. An unexplained fact has often been regarded as a miracle by those who have believed in miracles: Rip van Winkle might well have described as a miracle the voice and the music emanating from a portable wireless set. The advance of science, based on presupposing the uniformity of nature, has seriously impaired the credibility of miracles; for example, few educated people can now believe that the sun went backward ten degrees as a sign to King Hezekiah. If, however, the Old Testament nature miracles are rejected, then by parity of reasoning those in the New Testament must be rejected also. This was where Strauss gave the greatest offence, for he argued that the New Testament miracles are mythical, and that the accounts of them were based on Old Testament parallels. The Messiah had to work miracles as Moses and Elijah had done, and even greater miracles than those.

Lessing quotes[1] Michaelis's *Introduction to the New Testament* as follows: 'The miracles by which the Christian religion is confirmed would prove its truth just as well even though the witnesses were not inspired but purely human witnesses. The miracles being true, the discourses so confirmed become the infallible word of God.' Michaelis had abandoned verbal inspiration, but he still

[1] *Axiomata*—edn cit, viii, p. 199.

held that it is miracle which proves the truth of Christianity. 'Orthodox Christians from Aquinas' to the seventeenth century 'aways affirmed that the biblical miracles were the rational guarantees of the truth of the Scriptural revelation.'[1] This view was slow to vanish from Germany and slower still from England. Even when miracles were no longer regarded as the prime evidence for Christianity, they were still thought, as for instance by Mansel (Dean of St Paul's 1868–71), to be 'an essential part of Christianity'.[2]

Today the situation seems to be different. Many theologians reject the Virgin Birth; but although 'I would never believe in the Divinity of Christ because of the Virgin Birth, I believe in the Divinity on the grounds of Christ's moral claims upon the Disciples, and upon us, and then I would see a miraculous birth as congruous'.[3] It is true that the Archbishop thinks that the historical evidence for the Virgin Birth is good; others have found it negligible. But once we begin to ask what is 'congruous' we are on the slippery slope which leads, as Strauss would say, to myths. What, save congruity, can be urged in favour of the Immaculate Conception and the Bodily Assumption? Depart from historical evidence and a scientific conscience, and you have delivered yourself to either authority or infidelity.

However that may be, it seems that much modern apologetic is disposed to 'soft-pedal' the miraculous. Its task is perhaps to gain a hearing for religion in an age which has so largely turned away from it. One way of dealing with the matter, however, which is philosophically up to date, is contained in an Oxford Inaugural Lecture by the present Bishop of Durham. In *Miracles, an Exercise in Logical Mapwork* (Oxford, 1952), Dr Ian Ramsey examines the 'broad characteristics of the languages of natural science, of history and metaphysics', and asks 'whether a place can be found anywhere, and, if so, in what sort of setting, for the word "miracle"'. The result of the inquiry is to show that the questions that may be usefully asked about a miracle are not scientific at all.

That the word 'miracle' can occur in the language of science only as a word descriptive of a delusion may be obvious enough. But preoccupation with the ways in which people use language is

[1] A. Richardson: *History Sacred and Profane* (London, 1964), p. 21.

[2] Quoted here from R. W. Mackay: *The Tübingen School* (London, 1863), p. 164.

[3] Archbishop A. M. Ramsey in *What is a Christian?* p. 5, in Television Rediffusion, 1. xii, 1966.

apt to blind the eye to the things which in language we describe. Scientific method presupposes the uniformity of nature, but it abstracts from our experience of reality. The beauty of nature and art is outside its purview. Miracle, therefore, is a problem, not for science but for history. F. H. Bradley, in his *Presuppositions of Critical History* (Oxford, 1874) was clearly concerned with this problem. He had read, and been influenced by, F. C. Baur and the other Tübingen theologians. But he was also unable to extricate himself from the positivism of his day, and therefore he had to reject an alien element (e.g. a miracle) which 'we cannot recognize as akin to ourselves' (i.e. as scientists) (p. 32). 'There may be events which though in themselves coming under the conditions of history can yet be supported by no analogy from present experience and, despite their testimony, they must wait for further experience' (pp. 40–1). (Query: another Resurrection.) But 'it would be a serious mistake to suppose, because at a certain time criticism is not justified in considering an event historical, that *therefore* criticism will *never* be able to affirm it' (pp. 58–9). But the critical historian is always to keep on the side of safety. 'It is better to suspend the judgment and be wrong, than to be right against reason and in the face of science' (p. 59).

This is where Bradley lapses into positivism and where his essay fails to convince. For science, miracles cannot happen. But history may be unable to give an account of an event without seeing it as real, even if for science it is inexplicable, or at least unexplained. And the historian's account may be the only one which can make subsequent events explicable. This might be true of the Resurrection.[1]

Unless what I have just said provides an answer, Strauss on this question of miracle has not been answered. But one of his critics did by implication raise the question which was to be, and perhaps is still, a vital one: 'If Christ professed to work miracles, and wrought them not, what warrant have we for the trustworthiness of his other teaching?'[2] (The statement that Jesus 'professed' to work miracles may perhaps have its justification in Luke vii. 22.) The answer could only come from the radical examination, sifting, and criticism of the New Testament.

[1] What I have been doing in this paragraph is defending my assertion that miracle is not to be dismissed *a priori*. I am not trying to defend miracle or any particular miracle. For my distinction between science and history I rely on the works of R. G. Collingwood and I accept this distinction from him.

[2] Mansel again, quoted in R. W. Mackay, *op. cit.*, p. 157.

Strauss's book was greeted with execration, but it was not answered. On its own ground it was unanswerable; much of it is unanswerable still on any ground. But theologians who were open-minded enough to take it seriously saw that the only way to an answer was through a critical examination of the biblical writings, especially those of the New Testament. This task was undertaken by Strauss's own teacher at Tübingen, F. C. Baur. Ten years after the publication of Strauss's *Life*, Baur published his book on St Paul. 'The outcry against Strauss simply showed the necessity of going deeper still and more thoroughly into the critical process which he began.'[1]

Baur proceeded to examine the books of the New Testament, beginning with the Epistles of St Paul which, he realized, were the oldest. For various reasons he doubted the authenticity of some of the Epistles, but regarded Galatians, Romans, and I and II Corinthians as certainly genuine.[2]

It follows that the first half of Acts cannot be accepted as historical. Contradictions between it and what Paul wrote cannot be explained away, except at the expense of Paul's moral character. Moreover, the quarrel between Paul and the Jerusalem Church of James and Peter, so evident in the Epistles, is minimized in Acts. This may be an attempt to reconcile the Jersusalem Church with Paul's churches, and this reconciliation may have been necessary for the success of Christianity.

What Christians did Paul persecute? He was a Pharisee, but there does not seem to have been any quarrel between the Pharisees and the original Disciples. The latter attended the synagogue and kept the Jewish feasts. They were a Judaic sect.

Stephen, however, was a Hellenist, and there were 'murmurings of the Grecians against the Hebrews' (Acts vi. 1). The Twelve attempted to settle the matter by giving a commission to seven men, all with Greek names, and Stephen was one. In due course he was accused of uttering blasphemous words against Moses. The speech which he made in his defence may well have been responsible for Paul's conversion, for Paul must have reflected on similar lines. The Jews were apostate, slayers of the prophets, and now of Jesus, whose coming the prophets had foretold. The

[1] Eng. tr., London and Edinburgh, 1876, i, p. 3.

[2] This view, with the aid of a computer, has been defended by Mr A. Q. Morton in *Christianity and the Computer*, published with Mr. J. McLeman in 1964. My doubts about the computer as an instrument of literary research have been printed in *Svensk Exegetisk Årsbok*, xxviii–xxix, 1963–4, pp. 111–16.

Temple is not the dwelling-place of the Most High. But this implies that the absolute importance of Judaism is at an end, and the Mosaic law is no more than a schoolmaster to bring us to Christ.

Paul was an educated man and a thinker; he was brought up amongst Gentiles in an Hellenistic environment; he was also a man of force and fire, energetic, dogmatic, a skilful teacher. Whatever happened to him on the road to Damascus (and the accounts of that episode vary), he became convinced that he had received a special revelation. He emphasizes that what he teaches was not derived from the Twelve, or from anyone else. It came to him direct from Heaven.

His faith is rooted in Judaism: e.g. he believes in an imminent second coming of the Messiah; he believes in demons influencing human affairs. But his differences from Judaism are profound and vital.[1] Righteousness, or justification, is not by keeping the law or by doing good works; it is by faith alone. Faith in the atoning death of Jesus reconciles us to God; and because Jesus lives we shall live also. In Christ there is neither Jew nor Greek. This is Paul's universalism, the rock of offence to the Jerusalem church.

Baur expounds Paul with care, sympathy, and at great length. His book ought to be required reading in all theological colleges, where reasons may be found for accepting what Paul does positively believe. I have not been able to find many of them myself.

Some things are clear. Paul knows nothing of a Virgin Birth, or of an empty tomb, or of the gift of the Spirit at Pentecost, or of the doctrine of the Trinity. He was acquainted with some of the teaching of Jesus but he is strangely indifferent to it, as well as to the events of Jesus's life, although it must be admitted that much of the moral teaching of Jesus is concentrated, without any mention of him, in Romans xii and Philippians iv. It is the death of Jesus on which his soteriological faith rests. Allied with this is a sacramentalism without which his preaching to the Gentiles would have been vain. Sacramental cults were common in the regions of Paul's success. Paul may have been responsible for the division of the Bible into the Old Testament and the New. It is not always appreciated that 'Testament' means 'covenant', and the belief

[1] Professor Black points out to me that the differences are from Pharisaic Judaism, but much less from Qumran Judaism. For Paul's belief in demonic powers, see S. G. F. Brandon: *The Trial of Jesus of Nazareth* (London, 1968), pp. 14–16.

that God made a covenant with Abraham, or anyone else, is not easy of acceptance.

Baur's work made a considerable stir, but it was not translated into English until 1876. Meanwhile, however, biblical criticism had begun to make progress in England. Benjamin Jowett, whose edition of *Thessalonians, Galatians, and Romans* got him into serious trouble in 1855 because he was unsound on the doctrine of the Atonement, gave further offence five years later when, in his essay on the *Interpretation of Scripture*, he asserted that the Bible was to be studied like any other book. This had been said before,[1] but Jowett was a clergyman of the Church of England, and he was indicted for heresy, for teaching what conflicted with the Thirty-nine Articles. The prosecution was withdrawn, but it is interesting to note that Tractarians and Evangelicals alike were still convinced in 1860 of the inerrancy of Scripture and its plenary inspiration. Nearly thirty years afterwards this was still Liddon's position. He declared that the names of Pharoah's magicians, Jannes and Jambres, were divinely guaranteed through their mention by St Paul, and must consequently be accepted as historical by all true Christians.[2]

In 1862 Colenso, a Bishop in South Africa, gave rise to an even greater storm by his book on the Pentateuch. As a Fellow of St John's College, Cambridge, he had been a mathematician, and he applied his mathematical mind to the Pentateuchal arithmetic. A. P. Stanley, then an Oxford Professor, regarded the book as decisive against supposing that belief in the exactness of the numbers in the Old Testament, and in the Mosaic authorship of the Pentateuch, was essential to revelation. Yet he looked on the book as a mistake, because it would fix public attention on mere defects of structure and detail, and so lead the public to throw out the baby with the bath water.[3] Stanley was a liberal, and his acceptance of Colenso's argument was not widely shared in ecclesiastical circles. The Bishop of Cape Town excommunicated Colenso, but the law courts confirmed him in his See in 1866. Once again, as in 1864 when 'Hell was dismissed with costs',[4] the law courts proved themselves to be more enlightened than Pusey and his friends and allies.

[1] By Lessing (see above, Ch. 3) whom Jowett had studied and whom he quotes in this essay.

[2] Quoted by N. P. Williams in *Northern Catholicism*, p. 144.

[3] R. E. Prothero: *Life of A. P. Stanley* (London, 1893), ii, pp. 100–4

[4] G. Faber: *Life of Jowett* (London, 1957), pp. 272–6.

In 1678 Richard Simon was expelled from his Order, and his *Histoire critique du Vieux Testament* was burnt, because he had ventured to say that 'Moise ne peut être l'auteur de tous les livres qui lui sont attribués'. Two centuries later, the General Assembly of the Free Church of Scotland found that Robertson Smith, Professor of Hebrew in that Church's College in Aberdeen, was heretical for saying the same thing. As one of his accusers put it: 'Professor Smith says that Moses did not write Deuteronomy. This is equivalent to saying that it is a fraud and a fabrication.'[1] Smith's persecution began in 1875, after the publication of his article 'Bible' in the *Encyclopaedia Britannica*. Proceedings against him dragged on until May 1880, when he was admonished and told to behave better in future. Further offence was given, however, by his article on 'Hebrew Language and Literature', and new proceedings started, culminating in his dismissal from his Chair in 1881.

Since this was the last heresy case which concerned the Pentateuch, it may be worth taking a look at the doctrine of verbal inspiration which held the field so long, and which appears, in some quarters, to hold the field still. This is a doctrine which the Thirty-nine Articles do not teach, although, as we have seen, it was widely held in the Anglican Church in the sixties. So far as the Old Testament is concerned, the Robertson Smith case, and his writings, may have done something to dissolve it. In Scotland, however, the phraseology of the Westminster Confession, which has not yet fallen into desuetude, is far more definite: 'For the better preserving and propagating of the truth, it pleased God to commit the same unto writing, which maketh the Holy Scripture to be most necessary. All books of the Old and New Testaments are given by the inspiration of God to be the rule of faith and life. . . . The authority of the Holy Scripture dependeth not upon the testimony of any man or church but wholly upon God . . . and therefore it is to be received because it is the word of God.' The phraseology may possibly permit of a latitudinarian interpretation, and such an interpretation may be current today, but it certainly was rejected by Smith's accusers.

In other quarters it appears to be rejected still. In 1893 Pope Leo XIII issued an encyclical which allowed no latitude at all, but reaffirmed the complete inerrancy of the Bible. Some ten years

[1] J. S. Black and G. W. Chrystal: *Life of Robertson Smith* (London, 1912), pp. 287, 280.

later, the Pontifical Biblical Commission required Roman Catholics to believe, or at least not to question, the Mosaic authorship of the Pentateuch, and much else that most biblical scholars would now decline to affirm.[1]

This doctrine of verbal inspiration or biblical inerrancy is so strange that it is difficult to understand how any reasonable man ever came to believe it. Perhaps it is easy to say this after a century of biblical criticism and after we have become accustomed to think of the Bible, not as *a* mere book, but as a collection of books. To think of it as a collection, however, readily raises in our minds the question: Who made the collection, why, and when? We then recall Lessing's remark that Christianity existed before the New Testament was written, and we can infer that it was the Church that made the Bible, and not vice versa. The New Testament canon may not have been finally settled until AD 692.[2] Hence the doctrine of inerrancy or verbal inspiration rests on the authority of the Church, and belief in the doctrine appears to be forced on those who accept that authority. The Reformers differed from the Roman Church only in preferring the Hebraic to the Alexandrian canon, and so in rejecting the canonicity of the Apocrypha. Acceptance of the authority of the Church may be consequential on the belief, which I cannot share, that the (Roman) Church was founded by Jesus Christ and that he promised that it would be guided by the Spirit into all truth. Some may find it reasonable to follow Newman rather than Strauss. But I am not one of the 'some'.

If the Robertson Smith case did result in leaving Old Testament scholars free to pursue their critical inquiries without fear of prosecution, it became clear in 1889 that the same battle had to be won in relation to the New Testament. In his essay in *Lux Mundi*, Charles Gore, a young Anglo-Catholic leader, clearly accepted the principle of criticism for the New Testament as well as for the Old. His was an endeavour 'to bring the Christian creed into its right relation to the modern growth of knowledge'.[3] There was a considerable outcry from the older Tractarians, but Gore's 'Liberal Catholicism' carried the day with the younger men and liberated them from the shackles of an infallible book.

[1] A. R. Vidler: *Church in an Age of Revolution* (Penguin Books, 1961), p. 187. But the best source for all this is Loisy's *Mémoires*.

[2] So N. P. Williams in *Northern Catholicism*, p. 165.

[3] Quoted from W. J. Sparrow Simpson in *Northern Catholicism*, p. 64.

Gore and his friends thought that, if critical methods were rightly applied to the New Testament, the full historicity of the Gospels stood up to the test. He persisted in this view for the rest of his long life. The young radical came to be regarded as hopelessly conservative. In 1889 he did not realize what floodgates he was opening. Loisy was already at work.

In the Roman Church, as well as in the Scottish and the Anglican, there were, towards the end of the nineteenth century, those who wished to come to terms with the 'growth of modern knowledge'. It is true that the Roman Catholics were a very small minority, and they laboured under exceptional difficulties owing to the authoritarian character of their Church, and the recently decreed infallibility of the Pope. Nevertheless, they recalled Galileo's *eppur si muove*, and believed that the truth could not remain concealed or fail to prevail. They deserve crdit for their courage.

Alfred Loisy was one of those frail men who sometimes live to a great age. He was eighty-three when he died in 1940. He began his professorial work in a Catholic Institute in Paris with lectures on the Old Testament. In 1893 he was deprived of his Chair, but he was allowed to pursue and publish his researches, and to continue to officiate as a priest. His defence of the Roman Catholic Church against Harnack in 1897 got him into further trouble because of his heterodox views on what Jesus taught. He continued to publish commentaries, now on the books of the New Testament, each more radical than its predecessor, and it may not be surprising that he was excommunicated in 1908. He became a lay Professor in the Sorbonne, and lapsed further and further into infidelity. He summed up his work on Christian origins in 1933, when he published his book on *The Birth of Christianity*.

The book is very unsatisfying. It might be regarded as a manifesto of positivism. It cannot be treated seriously as history. However distinguished Loisy was as a philologist, he had little historical sense, and it is a misfortune that L. P. Jacks spent his declining years translating this book, when instead he might have translated at least the first two volumes of Loisy's three-volume masterpiece, his own *Mémoires*. This autobiography, written in beautiful and limpid French, is not only the story of his own gradual loss of faith, his struggles with the Roman authorities, and the attempts of scholars like Archibishop Mignot and Baron von Hügel to help him, but also the history of the rise, decline, and fall of the Modernist movement in the Roman Catholic Church. The third volume, which deals with the lay period after 1908, is dry and spiritless.

In the years preceding his excommunication, Loisy was adopting a position very like tht of Hegel, Strauss, and, to quote another example, Francis Newman, one of the Cardinal's brothers, who had said: 'We find in historical religion two incongruous elements, iron and miry clay. The iron is the pure moral and spiritual doctrine. . . . The miry clay is the historical element.'[1] For Loisy the miry clay was there in what Jesus taught, the proclamation of the imminent coming of the Messiah and the Kingdom of God. But this was only the form in which the message had originally to be received: the message had to be preserved, expressed, and developed in the Church with its hierarchy, dogma, and worship. 'Jesus expected the Kingdom, and what came was the Church.' By 1908 Loisy had dissolved away almost everything in the New Testament except what Strauss had seen as historically certain, the apocalyptic or eschatalogical prophecy. And yet he was so enthralled by the Catholic ritual. and especially the Mass, that he could not see why, despite his historical disbeliefs, he should not be allowed to continue to celebrate.

Loisy seems to have had a logical but rather dry mind. He is quick to find interpolations in the Epistles and elsewhere where the argument seems to break. If he had been the author of the New Testament books, he would have written them more logically, more unambiguously, more clearly, more consistently, because, whatever else he was, he was a master of style, like Strauss. But he never seems to realize that his type of mind was not that of the Evangelists or Paul. He seems to have *a priori* canons of judgment about what is authentic and what is not (e.g. his selection of those verses in Acts iv which are authentic and which are not).[2] His judgment often strikes one as purely arbitrary: for example, 'from a story in Acts, superficially clear and deliberately confused, it follows that', etc. How does he know that it was *volontairement embrouillé*?[3] To make Paul a pupil of Gamaliel was as fictitious as the discourse of Gamaliel in chapter five and the charge against the Disciples (pp. 160 and 147). Only if Loisy possessed a second sight that worked backwards could we rely on this *ex cathedra* discrimination between fact and fiction in Acts.

[1] *The Soul* (London, 1905), p. 327.
[2] *Naissance du Christianisme*, p. 133, fn. 1.
[3] Acts vi, 1–6. *Naissance*, p. 140.

I have been as bored with Loisy (except in his *Mémoires*) as George Eliot was with Strauss. Despite what I have said about the general character of his work, there was a sentimental streak in him, and this may be responsible for his high regard for Rénan and for his omission of Strauss from his bibliography in *Naissance*. He seems to have had few followers, although I suppose that Guignebert, who shares his lack of historical sense, may be one. But one hint of Loisy's has been taken up in quarters where most of his findings are repudiated. 'The Gospels', he says, 'are not, properly speaking, historical documents, but liturgical catechisms.' This has been welcome to some Form-Critics and other dogmatic theologians.

Loisy's work does not seem to have made any lasting impact in these islands; indeed, his best work, his *Mémoires*, has apparently made none. His writings up to about 1920 did arouse interest in many quarters, but the interest seems to have died away. In the book to which I have referred already, Bishop Neill does not mention Loisy at all.

It was only when the influence of Hegel and F. C. Baur was waning in Germany that it began to register in these islands, and this is not the only instance of powerful continental work gaining new life here when it was dying at home. The case is different, however, with a remarkable book, first published in Germany in 1906, and first translated into English in 1910. I refer to Albert Schweitzer's *Quest of the Historical Jesus* (to quote the inspired title chosen by the English translator for *Von Reimarus zu Wrede*)—a book most germane to our inquiry.

CHAPTER 8

FROM SCHWEITZER TO FORM-CRITICISM

Schweitzer's great book, *von Reimarus zu Wrede*, is too well known in the English translation, *The Quest of the Historical Jesus*, for me to attempt any summary of its contents and results. I need only refer to his extraordinary command of his material, namely the literature of the Quest, almot wholly German (as he points out, although he devotes a chapter to Rénan), from the mid-eighteenth century to the end of the nineteenth. Schweitzer had himself so deeply studied the New Testament that he knew where the shoe pinched. He knew what questions to ask, and one by one the various lives which he examines fall by the wayside.

His book appeared in 1906. In 1913 he published what was called a second edition, but was almost a new book, as the new title *Geschichte der Leben-Jesu-Forschung* indicated. It is half as long again as the earlier work. It has never been translated into English and seems to be comparatively unknown here. It is therefore from this that most of what I have to say about Schweitzer is derived.

In the *first* place, he makes a far more exhaustive examination of Jewish apocalyptic in order to show how much of it Jesus adopted and how far, by his original genius, he adapted and altered it. This examination a modern scholar would take further in the light of the Dead Sea Scrolls.[1] *Secondly*, he assesses in detail, and with remarkable sympathy, the arguments of Drews and others who tried to show that Jesus never existed. Schweitzer summarizes Drews as follows: The life of Jesus, as sketched by the Synoptists, merely expresses in the guise of history the metaphysical ideas, the religious hopes, and the experiences of the community founded on Jesus as God of the cult. . . . The differences and contradictions in the Gospels are just expressions of the stages through which the Messiah concept developed in different communities at different times. Drews ignores Jewish apocalyptic, but tried to derive Christianity from gnosticism and oriental myths. For example, the Lamb of God, Agnus Dei, was originally Agni Deus, Agni being an Indian god of fire. In reply to all this, Schweitzer simply points out that Drews fails to explain how Christianity originated. How did it ever come to tie itself to a person? True, Drews ascribes Christianity to St Paul, but the

[1] See e.g. M. Black: *The Scrolls and Christian Origins* (Edinburgh, 1961).

evidence for Paul's existence is no better than that for the existence of Jesus, and even if he did exist, how does Drews, on his own principles, know that Paul really was the author of the Epistles ascribed to him? (p. 484).[1]

Anyone who is still disposed to think that Jesus was a myth may be referred to what seem to be Schweitzer's last and unanswerable words on the matter in his autobiography.[2]

Thirdly, if Jesus was not a myth, neither was he, as Bousset supposed, a symbol. 'How could a man be enriched, advanced in his inner life, lifted in his outer life above everything tragic and difficult, by a symbol? If the heart of religion is that it redeems us from the world, in that it makes us free from the passing hour, how could a man be saved better by a symbol than by his own rational religiousness? . . . A Jesus who in the last resort is a symbol with more or less reality is a matter of indifference to faith. A symbol brings nothing new to the life and content of religion' (p. 524).

If we approach the New Testament as historians, we cannot escape from what Strauss said and what Schweitzer worked out in detail: Jesus believed that the end of the world was nigh, and that the Kingdom of God was to be established in the lifetime of some of those to whom he spoke. This belief was falsified by events, but Paul still held it, and the initial success of the followers of Jesus and Paul is only to be explained by their readiness to accept this belief. Christianity, as distinct from Paul's universalistic Judaism, seems to have been invented by the author of the fourth Gospel.

The teaching of Jesus, however, Schweitzer continues, was not confined to declaring the nearness of the Kingdom of God. It was also ethical. Unless your righteousness is greater than that of the Scribes and Pharisees, ye shall in no wise enter the Kingdom of Heaven. Love your neighbour. The emphasis is on motive, and the motive must be love of God and your neighbour. It is true that this is accompanied, in the Sermon on the Mount, and elsewhere, with other teaching. The world and all its ties, even the nearest, are to be renounced. This, in Schweitzer's view, is an ethics *ad interim*, i.e. for the very short period that is to elapse before the Kingdom comes, in which all property ties are to disap-

[1] Unless otherwise stated, the page references are to the *Geschichte der Leben-Jesu-Forschung*.

[2] *Aus meinem Leben und Denken* (Leipzig, 1932), pp. 108–11.

pear, and where there is to be neither male nor female. Thus the ethical teaching is bound up with apocalyptic and eschatology.

In 1913, however, Schweitzer wrote: 'If Jesus came back, he would not speak in terms of late Jewish eschatology, but he would not change the fundamental character of his ethics. He would still teach us that we cannot enter the Kingdom of Heaven unless our righteousness is greater than that of the Scribes and Pharisees' (p. 596). Yet he says repeatedly that the ethics of Jesus cannot be separated from the eschatology or apocalyptic, and he means that it is a mistake to select some of the ethical teaching as genuine and to discard the rest as part and parcel of Judaic apocalyptic. This is to do violence to the evidence. 'We must', he says, 'accept the fact that the oldest records about Jesus are mingled with much that is miraculous, unclear, foreign to our ideas. A clear separation of what belongs to history and what arose from primitive misunderstandings, embellishment, and imaginary explanations is simply not possible' (pp. 554–5 fn.). 'The real Jesus may prove to be so conditioned by his age in his whole world of ideas that our relation to him becomes a problem' (p. 515). 'Christology has had little to say about the historical Jesus. It generally says that he revealed God as our Father, but is our conception of God the same as his? He seems to have held that God was not the Father of all men, but only of the predestined' (pp. 520–1). Therefore 'theology must choose between an unhistorical Jesus (Drews's myth) and an all too historical Jesus (i.e. a victim of Jewish apocalytic). *Tertium non datur*' (p. 518).

The historical Jesus, so far from being omniscient, was in fact in error. He announced the imminent appearance of a supernatural Kingdom of God. It did not appear. What, then, is his relevance for us today?

'Jesus means something to our world because a mighty spiritual force streams forth from him and flows through our time also. . . . It is the solid foundation of Christianity' (*Quest*, p. 397). He clothed his message in forms that we have outgrown, but the message can still be discerned. How? By what criterion are we to distinguish between permanent content and a purely dated form? Schweitzer's answer in 1913 is of great interest.

'Modern Christianity must from the start and always reckon with the possibility of an eventual sacifice of the Jesus of history. His significance should not be raised to the point of referring all knowledge back to him and building religion Christocentrically.

The Lord can always be only an element in religion; he ought never to be given out as its foundation. . . . Religion must have at its disposal a metaphysic, i.e. a fundamental insight into the essence and meaning of Being, an insight totally independent of history and tradition. . . . Otherwise religion is the slave of history' (p. 512). 'Theological history, like the infantry, cannot advance in the battle unless the artillery, the philosophy of religion, has done its work ahead of it' (p. 598). 'Jesus can be as little the basis of our ethics as of our religion. He can afford only one element, though a powerful and determining one' (p. 596). In other words, philosophy is to provide the criterion for sifting the teaching of the Gospels.

Whether Schweitzer continued to maintain this position is not clear. In his autobiography, published some twenty years later, he seems to take a different line: 'What grips us in the historical Jesus is his subordination to God. In this he stands out greater than the dogmatic personality of Christ conceived in accordance with Greek metaphysics as omniscient and free from error (edn. cit., p. 47). Liberal Christianity still has the spirit of Jesus on its side. . . . He did not ask his hearers to sacrifice thinking to believing. . . . In the messianic hope which his hearers carried in their hearts, he kindled the fire of an ethical faith. The Sermon on the Mount is the incontestable charter of liberal Christianity. . . . The religion of love which Jesus taught has been stripped of the dogmatic character that it had when it was expressed in terms of Jewish apocalyptic. The mould has been broken. Now we are justified in letting the religion of Jesus come alive in our thinking in its immediate spiritual and ethical essential character. . . . We adhere to those who believe that they serve Christianity better by the strength of surrender to Jesus's religion of love than by subjection to all the creeds' (*ibid.*, pp. 48–9). We are now to do what Schweitzer had once regarded as impossible, namely, to strip the teaching of Jesus from the husk of both Judaic apocalyptic and orthodox dogmatics, and here I cannot but agree with him.

In 1913 there was a contradiction, which critics of Schweitzer have not been slow to emphasize. What is the connection between the spirit of Jesus which drove Schweitzer out to become a medical missionary in Africa, and the historical Jesus which he himself depicted? Can '*tertium non datur*' be correct if the call to service in Africa was so strong? He ended his book in 1906, and preserved this in 1913, with the remark that the quest for the historical Jesus ended with a negative. For him, this seems to have been true. After examining all the permutations of attempts to read the riddle of the New Testament, he advances his own. But it collapses like the rest. He says himself that 'the riddle of the missing connection between the Synoptics and the Epistles remains the same, whichever of the two is supposed to be earlier' (p. 550). He admits that, even in his own account of Mark and Matthew, some things remain inexplicable.

Nevertheless, like Reimarus and Strauss, Schweitzer is a landmark. Subsequent attempts to deal with the problem of the historicity of the New Testament should begin from him. Some theologians take a new line altogether and try to begin with St Paul, as we shall see, but this leads to new difficulties. Schweitzer had genius; as well as musician, missionary, doctor, theologian, he was a great historian. In this respect he towers over successors who try to evade history by claiming that some historical statements in the creeds are really supra-historical, or else irrelevant to the proclamation of the Christian message.

At the end of the nineteenth century it must have looked as if the Modernist or Liberal battle was being won. In spite of opposition in some quarters, biblical criticism, sometimes radical, was proceeding. Liberal ideas were spreading amongst educated people, and some theologians of distinction were sitting lightly to orthodoxy. In 1890 Otto Pfleiderer published his book on the *Development of Theology in Germany and Great Britain in the Nineteenth Century*. His last chapter sketches the advance of biblical criticism, and it ends with the sentence: 'The days of a Newman and a Pusey are forever past for Oxford and for England.' No prophecy could have seemed more reasonable. None could have been more false.

It is worth remembering, however, that it is not only in theology that the decline of liberalism since 1900 has been perceptible. 'Who in 1900 could have predicted all the vicious and tawdry machinery of totalitarianism—systematic brain-washing, slanted propaganda, and down-grading of truth and freedom to mere counters in the political power-game, the contemptuous dismissal of all honest intellectual endeavour?'[1]

By 1910 Modernism had been stamped out in the Roman Church. A little earlier (1903) the Scottish *Encyclopaedia Biblica* was bitterly attacked as being too extreme. The temper of the time may be inferred from a comment by the able authors of Robertson

[1] Adapted from an anonymous review in *T.L.S.*, August 24, 1967.

Smith's *Life* in 1912: 'No repetition of the Smith case is now conceivable. But if anyone wishes a ready means of realizing for himself what the then new Deuteronomy heresy meant to the old orthodoxy, he has only to ask himself what would now be likely to happen in any Scottish church to any responsible person who should venture to signify his acceptance of . . . the analogous critical position now so widely accepted on certain New Testament questions such as . . . the authorship and date of the various writings attributed . . . to St John.'[1]

This may be too pessimistic. Questions of authorship and date may be left to scholars. It is when doctrinal inferences are drawn from answers to such questions that trouble arises. In 1898 there was founded in the Anglican Church a Society, later called the Modern Churchmen's Union. Publications by its members gave rise to some alarm from 1910 onwards, but the Union persevered, despite the conservative reaction, and in August 1921 its Conference in Cambridge produced headlines in the newspapers and long reports of the proceedings.

If any modern 'inquisitor of heretical pravity' peruses these proceedings today, he will suffer some disappointment. They are far less sensational and heretical than they were made out to be at the time. Nevertheless, there was voiced at this Conference an heretical interpretation of the Divinity of Christ. Jesus, it was maintained, was divine only in the sense that he was a perfect man; thus he differed from the rest of us only in degree and not in kind. This was an attempt to explain the two natures in Jesus, which had been a cardinal tenet of orthodoxy, but the attempt had to be repudiated. To deny the uniqueness of Christ was to depart from Christianity altogether.

The 1921 Conference was the last blaze of the candle before it went out, although in 1967, when Canon H. W. Montefiore speculated on the sexual life of Jesus, there was some stir in the press. The fact remains that the Modern Churchmen's Union does not now include so many theologians of distinction as it did forty or fifty years ago.

Why did this whole Modernist or Liberal movement fizzle out? The best answer seems to be Loisy's own: 'Individuals cannot all see in time or adequately the necessity for a transformation; the mass of believers do not understand this necessity; their leaders neither wish nor dare to discuss it. A form of religion which still

[1] *op. cit.*, p. 451.

satisfies the bulk of its adherents cannot be made to become suddenly other than it is. If Judaism had reformed itself by sacrificing the letter of the law, suppressing its traditional observances, and changing itself into a universal Church, this would have looked like the suicide of the original religion. The Jews could scarcely wish to commit a suicide of this kind, even if it were an indispensable and certain condition of resurrection.'[1]

The writers we have been considering were theologians, but an important contribution to the subject of Christian origins was made by a distinguished historian of the ancient world, Eduard Meyer. The first two volumes of his *Ursprung und Anfänge des Christentums* appeared in 1921, the third in 1923 (Stuttgart and Berlin). It is the fact that he was a skilled historian which gives his book its interest; no doubt it is in certain respects out of date;[2] no doubt he ignores contributions to the subject from outside Germany; no doubt his utter contempt, even hatred, of the Anglo-Saxon world occasionally impairs his objectivity; but his book does not deserve to be forgotten. In some respects it was before its time. The appeal to history, which was becoming unheard in 1923, has been heard again in 1966 (see below, on *Vindications*). No English translation has appeared.

In the first place, as an historian, Meyer insists that Luke is another, and a great one at that. The third Gospel and Acts form one book. Like Thucydides, Luke wrote the speeches which he ascribes to others, but the content of them is as authentic as that in those of his ancient Greek predecessor (i, ch. 1).

Unlike the other Evangelists, Luke provides some dates. It is true that he gets some of these wrong, in particular by confusing the universal census of AD 74 with the partial one of AD 6. But he probably experienced the later one, and merely assumed that the earlier one was of the same character (*ibid.*). The chronology of Acts is correct; it can be verified from Tacitus, Josephus, *et al.* (iii, pp. 27–54).

It is true that Luke contradicts the other Synoptics in places, but what he is doing is thinking out what must have happened, and then altering the tradition accordingly. The account of the Ascension in Acts must be an interpolation (i. ch. 1), because it contradicts the Gospel. It is also true that Luke omits all sorts of things that we would like to know; but this is true of historians

[1] *La Religion d'Israel*, p. 295, slightly paraphrased.
[2] See S. Neill, *op. cit.*, p. 285.

generally; what is important to one generation is not to an earlier one (iii, pp. 12–14).

Acts is one-sided. What history is not? But the main outline of the development and spread of Christianity is clear and correct. It may seem to be contradicted by Paul's statements in the Epistles, but 'Paul was a politician through and through'. He therefore made compromises for the sake of getting on with his work. He circumcises Timothy to avoid trouble. He tells the Sanhedrin that he upholds the law. Inwardly his standpoint is not theirs, but he does not want to lose the support of the Jerusalem Church. He makes collections for it, despite whatever differences he had with Peter (iii, 64–71).

With Luke, then, as his main guide, Meyer proceeds with his historical task. He mentions Strauss once in passing (i, p. 281), Schweitzer never. He gives the general impression that he is more conservative than many theologians. The strength of his book is that he can draw on his wide knowledge of the history of the ancient world, and so can see the origin and growth of Christianity in its proper context.

The Virgin Birth, in his view, is a myth, like numerous Greek and Egyptian stories of divine parentage (i, pp. 55–8).

If anything is authentic in the story of Jesus it is the remark that he is 'beside himself' and 'a prophet has no honour in his own household'. This is just what one would expect. Parents would try to bring the 'prophet' back to a regular, sensible life (i, p. 70).

The sayings of Jesus about John the Baptist, and his reply to the Baptist's disciples, cannot be authentic. They imply that he is the Messiah, and this is what the Disciples and Paul believed only after his death. The Baptist was famous, and thus became suspect to Herod. The Jews regarded him, unlike Jesus, as a martyr for the Jewish religion (i, p. 87).

Twenty pages later, however, Meyer says that, after the Temptation in the wilderness, Jesus believed that he was the Messiah. When he said 'thy sins be forgiven thee' he was implying that he was the Messiah foretold by Daniel. Peter recognizes him as such, but is at once cursed because he thinks in terms of a worldly kingdom. Jesus regards himself as a suffering servant, but one who will return on the clouds of heaven at the end of the world. This the Disciples do not understand (i, pp. 106–22).

Mark xiii cannot be authentic. It is an eschatological tract, belonging to the first generation of Christians, and may be Pauline (i, pp. 125–30).

Meyer does not think that Jesus wanted to oppose the power of Rome. What he did oppose was the Jewish law, the priesthood and its powers.

The Jews wanted Barabbas freed because he was the leader of an insurrection. Jesus was only a preacher. True, there are signs of force, but this often happens with reformers. Their followers become over-enthusiastic (i, pp. 167–95).

The teaching of Jesus was meant for the Jews alone, and it consists merely in a re-interpretation of the law. Passages to the contrary cannot be authentic. Luke omits the injunction not to preach to the Gentiles, but he is an apologist for St Paul (i, p. 302). Despite his encomium on Luke as an historian, Meyer does not hesitate to reject his guidance when it conflicts with his own conception of what must have happened.

Christianity is a new religion which arose from the consequences of the teaching of Jesus, without and against his will (ii, p. 59).

The original group stick to the Messiah conception in Daniel and subsequent Jewish writings. Therefore Jesus is the son of David, intended by God from the beginning to be Redeemer and world-ruler, the son of God in closest connection with the Father.

No attempt was made to work out the connection of Father and Son, or to produce a dogmatic formula. It sufficed for the early Apostles that the Spirit, spoken of by God through the prophets, had entered Jesus at his baptism when, as later in the Transfiguration, a heavenly voice declared that he was the Son of God. This gave him power to fight and overcome the hostile powers of Satan and reveal to believers the true essence of the Father and the meaning of his commands.

After the Resurrection all power in heaven and earth is given to him; he is the vice-gerent of God, ruler of the world, and Lord; as such he would return in the immediate future from heaven to judge the quick and the dead in the way sketched in Daniel. Through him those who accepted his teaching and believed in him were brought into immediate relation with the Father and became sons of God, filled by God or by Christ with the same spirit which worked in Christ.

There the Jerusalem community stopped. It had a religion but no theology.

Jewish literature did have the conception of a pre-existent Son of Man, but this never appears in the Synoptics, still less his association with the Creation.

Theology begins with Paul, who attempts, with difficult mystical phraseology, to solve the insoluble problem. He goes on to ever greater intensification of Christ's likeness to God, until, in John, Jesus appears as the divine creative word, as the manifestation of God, as co-existent with God, and finally himself a God (iii, pp. 236–7).

Thus 'it cannot be too strongly stressed that the victory of Christianity is really the victory of heathenism'. After the teaching of the fourth Gospel (which was written for Christians—if Jesus had taught what it contains, he would have had few followers, i, p. 327) had elevated Jesus to the Godhead, the Marian cult was adopted, and eventually polytheism was restored by the cult of the Saints in the Roman Catholic Church (ii, 23).

The influence of Zoroaster on the development of Christianity is important. The Apocalypse is full of him, as well as of astrology and Greek myths. This is not surprising if it was written in the Near East, perhaps in Ephesus, but it is in crying contradiction with the historical Jesus and has nothing in common with him (i, p. 382). Luther on the devil might be Zoroaster *redivivus* (ii, p. 81).

We have already seen Hegel comparing and contrasting Jesus and Socrates, so Meyer's allusion to this topic may fitly conclude these extracts from his book. After the Crucifixion the Disciples were in despair. Soon they were full of hope. Other Jewish sects were full of enthusiasm, but they did not claim that the Messiah *had* come. The hope of the Disciples must have been due to the tremendous force of the personality of Jesus. He filled them with creative power despite and beyond his death. This has no parallel in world history. The nearest parallel is Socrates, whose influence was greatest after his undeserved death. On these two personalities rested the whole further development of the intellectual and spiritual life of western man (iii, p. 219).

These citations may convey something of the flavour of the book; but they may not adequately stress its range and its scholarship. On St Paul Meyer may owe more to Baur than he acknowledges. Later historical work has cast doubt on many of his conclusions, but the same is true of Gibbon, whom we still read with profit. He deserves to be read, even if only, unlike Baur, he writes vigorously and clearly. But although he tells us convincingly what Paul and the early Church believed, he does not help us to decide what it is reasonable for us to believe now.

The decline of Modernism was accompanied in Protestantism by a recrudescence of dogmatic theology. Karl Barth's *Commentary on Romans* was published in 1918. He accepts biblical criticism, although it may seem to an unsympathetic reader that he does not see the inroads which the criticism should make in his doctrine. He might almost have re-echoed Strauss and said that he restored dogmatically what he destroyed critically, only his restoration is all the greater, while his destruction is so much less. His disparagement of human reason cannot commend his work to a Gifford Lecturer (although he was one himself), and it is surprising that his authoritarian dogmatics were accepted so soon and by so many able Protestant theologians in so many countries. It was as if he had gone back to the Reformation and simply ignored nearly everything which has been the subject of the last five chapters, and yet his book on *Protestant Theology in the Nineteenth Century* (partially translated into English as *From Rousseau to Ritschl*) is full of sympathy, insight, and understanding.

While the Modernist movement failed, the historical questions which had given rise to it remained, though neglected. 'It has been possible so to conduct theological exposition of the Bible that questions of history are treated with less seriousness than is due to them.'[1] No doubt the questions have not been made easier with the lapse of time, but, as Schweitzer remarked (*Quest*, p. 116), 'there is no position so desperate that theology cannot find a way out of it'. The way out which has become popular in recent years is strange, but it cannot be ignored.

This trail seems to have been blazed so long ago as 1892 by M. Kähler in his book *Der sogennante historische Jesus und der geschichtliche biblische Christus*. The title cannot be translated; the distinction between *historische* and *geschichtliche* has no equivalent in English, and it has no foundation in German either.

Kähler's distinction is between the facts (these are past and dead) on the one hand, and, on the other, what is of lasting significance and speaks to the heart. The act of believing follows, not on reading about dead historical facts, but on acceptance of the preaching of the risen Lord.

[1] A. M. Ramsey: *From Gore to Temple* (London, 1960), p. 145.

Tillich in his introduction to the American translation[1] of this work speaks of 'the necessity to make the certainty of faith independent of the unavoidable incertitudes of historical research'. Apart from the word 'certainty', we hear at this point the voices of Lessing and Hegel, and of others much later. If we ask what the faith in the risen Lord is to be based on, how it is to come home to our minds, and not conflict with our reason, we are given answers indeed, but the partial, prejudiced, and ignorant historian cannot accept them.

Since Kähler seems to me to have been the inspiration of recent writers like Bultmann, Bornkamm, Käsemann, Fuchs, and others, I propose to dilate further on his book.

From beginning to end it is vitiated by his conception of history. It is positivistic, or, as Collingwood would have said, 'scissors and paste'. He possesses the faith, I do not know how. If scissors and paste history does not support it, this is because history of that kind cannot touch the faith. This is the *fons et origo* of the movement with which I am at present concerned, and this makes it all the more important to listen to what Kähler urges.

He holds that the biblical writings are historically valid as a document of the preaching which founded the Church, even though they cannot be accepted as historical documents for the course of the life of Jesus and of primitive Christianity (pp. 126, 136). But, we must reply, if the Gospels are the 'confessions' or 'testimonies' of believers in Christ and simply record what they did believe, what reason have we for accepting their beliefs? Perhaps it is a mistake, in Kähler's view, to ask for a reason, for he tells us that 'the purpose of the Gospels is to awaken faith in Jesus through a clear proclamation of his saving activity. . . . They are witnesses to something which lies beyond mere historical factuality, something we call revelation or salvation. . . . Thus regarded, they have a reliability which lies completely beyond proof and which would preclude the necessity of submitting them to a scientific test' (pp. 126, 127). Again one has to ask why we are to believe in a revelation beyond history and science, especially since most of those in the past who have believed in the revelation have supposed it to be based on and indispensably connected with 'historical factuality'.

[1] *The so-called Historical Jesus and the Historic Biblical Christ*, translated by C. E. Braaten (Philadelphia, 1964). My page references are to this edition.

Again, 'we see', Kähler tells us, a great difference between Paul, the disciple of the Pharisees, and the Master. On the one hand, the true Jew so profoundly and indelibly influenced by the cultural forces of his people and epoch; on the other, the Son of Man whose person and work convey the impression of one who lived, as it were, in the timeless age of the patriarchs. The Gospels confront us with an either-or. The question is whether the historian will humble himself before the unique sinless person (pp. 54–5). But what is the evidence for the unique sinless person, and is there not plenty of evidence that Jesus too was a true Jew, profoundly influenced, e.g. by Jewish messianic and apocalyptic ideas?

We are told further that we must grip the person and the work of Christ together. 'His work is his person in its historic-suprahistoric effect. To know this work in this sense, we do not need to be convinced by the methods of historical research. The work is accessible to us in the Church . . . in the confessing word and deed of our fellow Christians and in the living faith which Christ has evoked from us. The passionately held dogma about the Saviour vouches for the reliability of the picture transmitted to us by the biblical proclamation of Jesus as the Christ' (p. 95). This, however, is unconvincing. How can a passionately held dogma vouch for the reliability of an historical record?

Schweitzer never mentions Kähler's book, but he does deal (in his 1913 edition) with a book by G. Wobberminn[1] which starts from Kähler's fundamental distinction. Wobberminn, Schweitzer says (p. 521), 'wanders in dangerous ways when he tries to get round the historical problem by distinguishing between the *historisch* and the *geschichtlich* Jesus. The former is the person who appeared in Galilee and who is only vaguely known, and in whom therefore faith should not be placed.' 'The basis of [our] religion [according to Wobberminn] is the *geschichtlich* Jesus, the effective working of the historic personality, obvious in history up to the present time.' Now this is almost exactly Kähler's theory of the suprahistorical effect of Jesus, visible in the Church, etc. Schweitzer comments: 'This conjuring trick of modern scholaticism can contribute nothing to solving the problem. How can faith rest on what the historic personality has done in history since the first century AD? It is not difficult to show, when we come to examine the effects achieved in his name, and under his influence in the

[1] *Geschichte und Historie in Religions-Wissenschaft* (Tübingen, 1911).

Church or elsewhere, that along with much good they include great evils. What evils have not been done in his name?' This seems to me to be unanswerable. Kähler sees only what he is looking for. The attempt to rescue Christianity, and especially the life of Jesus, from historical criticism is a complete failure.

So I say. But some theologians disagree, and it would be unscholarly not to say something about them.

So long ago as the beginning of this century, Harnack held[1] that 'the whole of Jesus's message may be reduced to these two heads—God as the Father, and the human soul so ennobled that it can and does unite with him'. He went on to distinguish between the Easter message and the Easter faith. The former consists of alleged facts, the empty tomb and the post-Resurrection appearances; the latter is the conviction that the crucified one gained a victory over death. This faith we must cling to, even if the message is doubtful. But, if the message is doubtful, what is the reason for holding the faith?

Historical scepticism along with theological dogmatics has gone much further in the work of Barth, Brunner, Bultmann, and others.

Barth tells that we do not know either God or man apart from Christ who reveals the true nature of both God and man.[2] (This seems to be an underestimate of the Psalms and the Prophets.) But when we ask how the revelation of Christ is to be ascertained, we encounter a difficulty. The Gospels were not intended to be historical records. (Even if this were true, H. Conzelmann[3] is right to say that this is no reason why we should not be able to use them as historical records.) We cannot derive from them, Barth thinks, a life of Jesus or a reconstruction of his personality. What he taught is as irrelevant to us as it was to St Paul. It is only the eye of faith that can find a revelation of God in Jesus, and this faith is based on the miracles, the Resurrection, and its aftermath. If, however, the Gospels are evidence for these things, why are they not evidence for the teaching of Jesus too? The faith is left hanging in the air.

When Barth reads the Gospels, he finds the Rabbi of Nazareth, historically so difficult to get information about, and, when it is

[1] *What is Christianity?* (London, 1904), p. 65.

[2] Quoted here from W. Hordern in *Theologians of our Time*, ed. A. W. and E. Hastings (Edinburgh, 1966), p. 83.

[3] *R.G.G.*[3] III, article on *Jesus Christus*.

obtained, the Rabbi is apt to impress us as a little commonplace alongside more than one other founder of a religion, and even alongside many later representatives of his own religion.[1]

This is not Barth's last word, however. He holds that the revelation of God does not take place in history, but in a sort of supra-history which is exempt from all criticism by historians. This seems to be a reversion to Kähler, and not to be more intelligible. Barth apparently begins by accepting the teaching of St Paul, though the reasons for accepting it remain obscure. As Bultmann puts it, in criticizing Barth: 'How do these events come into the believer's field of vision? And how is such faith distinguished from a blind acceptance involving a *sacrificium intellectus*?'[2]

Brunner is no less radical. Faith does rest on the historicity of the Crucifixion and the Resurrection, but while the believer regards these facts as absolutely certain, for the historian they can be no more than probable. (Has any competent historian ever cast doubt on the Crucifixion?). The historian cannot disprove them, because they belong to a dimension which lies beyond the scope of historical investigation. Perhaps the meaning of this strange doctrine is something like the following: A scientific account of a sunset can take no account of its beauty, and yet the beauty may be the most significant thing about it. So too, the historian, faced with the Synoptic Gospels, may sift them and produce an intepretation of the history which they enshrine. But he must omit what is revealed there to the eye of faith. The meaning of the events escapes him.

This, however, is unconvincing. The methods of physical science depend on abstraction. The historian, on the other hand, deals with the concrete. The scientist does not dispute the reality of the sunset, although he has to abstract from its beauty, whereas the historian may find that he cannot interpret the evidence without discarding as myth what is alleged to be fact. There is no appeal, if an historical movement is being interpreted, from what the historian finds to something alleged still to be historical, but beyond the historian's competence. In so far as the historian misconceives or ignores the meaning and significance of the facts, he is failing as an historian; just as he fails if he starts with presuppositions, as for instance that miracle is impossible, which he fails to recognize or to discount.

[1] Quoted here from D. M. Baillie: *God was in Christ* (London, 1948), p. 12.
[2] *Essays Philosophical and Theological* (London, 1955), p. 261.

Dr Nathaniel Micklem offers a not dissimilar analogy: The historian will be able to ask why the artist came to paint his picture, or what caused the picture from the point of view of history; but a wise man will see more in the picture than the historian can tell him.[1] No doubt this is true. But the Gospels have every appearance of being historical documents, and have been used as such. Therefore they are within the historian's province. If instead they are works of art or catechisms, what becomes of the historicity in which Christianity is rooted?

Latterly, Bultmann may have been even more influential than Barth or Brunner. He is even more difficult to understand. He is associated with the word 'demythologizing'. Professor Ian Henderson, in his small but excellent book on Bultmann (London, 1965), traces Bultmann's use of myth to Eichhorn who interpreted the language of the Old Testament as that of a primitive people, unable to use abstract nouns, and ignorant of causes. Thus the changing thoughts of a man's mind are ascribed to a dialogue between himself and God. Cain kills Abel and thinks he will be asked where Abel is. He ascribes the question to God. When it is said that God appeared to a man in a dream, what is meant is that the man dreamt about God. Hence the Old Testament is myth and is to be interpreted as Homer and Hesiod are. Disbelief in nectar and ambrosia should imply disbelief in the tree of knowledge. You cannot have a real Eve and a figurative serpent.

When Bultmann applies a similar interpretation to the New Testament he is following Strauss, whom Professor Henderson does not mention. But the question obviously arises, if myth is the language of a primitive people, why is it still supposed to be the language of writers several centuries later?

If I understand Bultmann aright, most of what the Gospels contain is myth. 'For the New Testament writers the universe is a three-storeyed edifice . . . heaven, earth, and hell. . . . The earth is occupied by invading demons and spirits who may literally take possession of men. The world was regarded as in bondage to Satan. . . . This mythology is not only the background of the proclamation of the Gospel message but its presupposition. . . . This mythology is obsolete and incredible. . . . We must accept or reject the entire mythology.'[2] Bultmann rejects it, but this in no way impedes or

[1] *Christian Thinking To-day* (London, 1967), p. 108.
[2] Dr J. H. Thomas in *The Times*, May 18, 1968.

detracts from the faith—the faith, I must suppose, as promulgated by St Paul, or St John.

Faith, Bultmann holds, had nothing to do with historical probabilities but was a response to the word of God in the living present. Nothing historical was required except the fact that Jesus was crucified and was believed to have risen. *What* Jesus was it is impossible for history to ascertain. Christian faith is not a phenomenon of religious or cultural history. It is the answer to the word of the transcendent God that encounters man.[1] Paul claims direct revelation that the crucified Jesus has been raised from the dead and made Messiah. He is untouched by what Jesus taught. The latter is irrelevant to him (p. 186). But is it to us, who are not enslaved by Jewish messianic hopes? Moreover, Paul does refer, even though only occasionally, to the teaching of 'the Lord'.

Bultmann will not allow that Christianity stands or falls by New Testament criticism, his own Form-Criticism or any other. It depends on the proclamation of the Gospel, mainly in the Epistles and partly in Acts. The function of those passages in the Synoptics which can be accepted is purely ancillary.[2] What mystifies me is why we are expected to accept the proclamation once we have seen that so much in the Gospels, including apparently the Resurrection, is myth.[3]

This whole theological enterprise, which is based on believing the theology of St Paul, but on scepticism about the Gospels, even about the great miracles, must seem very odd to an historian. But there is an answer from Dr Alan Richardson, the Dean of York. The sort of history, he holds, which these eminent German theologians repudiate is the positivistic history, the sort of thing that Collingwood described as 'scissors and paste'. Give up this notion of history and adopt the methods, presuppositions, and outlook of modern historians, and the whole picture is transformed.[4]

The historian, Dr Richardson argues, lives in a 'climate of opinion' from which he cannot extricate himself. Climates change owing to changes in historical events. These changes lead the

[1] *Existence and Faith* (London, 1961), p. 288.

[2] I. Henderson, *op. cit.*, p. 18.

[3] I hope that I have not misrepresented Dr Bultmann. In conversation with him about his references to R. G. Collingwood in his Gifford Lectures, I could as little understand his answers as, I suppose, he did my questions. My treatment of these modern German theologians is indebted to Bishop Stephen Neill's book, which I have cited already, and also to an unpublished Ph.D. St Andrews thesis by W. B. Robinson.

[4] *History Sacred and Profane* (London, 1964).

historian to raise new questions about the past, so that there can never be any final, purely objective, history. There are facts in Luther's life on which all historians can agree; but the series of them is only chronicle and not history. History is the understanding of Luther's complex characer, and a Roman Catholic, a Protestant, and a free-thinker may all interpret the character diffently (pp. 202–3). The past is always an historical interpretation, and it is and must always be continually re-interpreted. This, however, is not a total relativism. 'When the twin bogeys of scientific objective history and "a nearly absolute relativism" have been laid, the way is open for the Christian understanding of the disclosure of God's purpose in history' (p. 259).

This is obscure, and it is not clarified by the further statement that 'there can be no . . . thinking about God's revelation in history which is not itself identified with an historical moment of encounter between the present and the past' (p. 261). A clue may perhaps be found in Dr Richardson's attitude to the Gospels. They are successive interpretations of the evidence for the life of Jesus (compare the views of Drews, see above p. 122). These interpretations are due to a deepening insight into what Jesus was and meant, and they are themselves mediated by the march of events. For example: 'The earliest generation of Christians were Jews of limited outlook. . . . It was inevitable that they should interpret the life and intention of Jesus Messiah in terms of their situation, and therefore in terms of his new return on the clouds of heaven. . . . The astonishing expansion of the Christian Church . . . in Rome . . . had already created an urgent need for a "new history", a thorough reappraisal of the meaning of the work and words of Jesus in the light of a new and unanticipated historical situation' (p. 236). 'The later rewriting of the Gospel story [in St John] may give us a profoundly illuminating representation of the truth of history. In this most important sense the Fourth Gospel is thoroughly historical' (p. 239).

While Dr Richardson's rejection of 'scientific history' and 'historical relativism' may be accepted, it seems to imply the scepticism about the historical Jesus which he criticizes in Barth, Brunner, and Bultmann. If contradictions in the Gospels are to be explained as due to different interpretations arising from diffeent historical circumstances, then they are evidence for what certain people believed at different times, and they will not provide evidence for enabling us to decide whether Jesus did say and mean that he 'was not sent but unto the lost sheep of the house of Israel', or whether he meant his gospel to be preached 'unto all nations'. The discourses in the Fourth Gospel are not a re-interpretation of the teaching of Jesus as reported in the Synoptics, but something different altogether. If there are agreed facts in a chronicle of Luther's life, what are the agreed facts in the chronicle of Jesus's life which are interpreted differently by different historians, especially the authors of the Gospels? Dr Richardson tells us that we must not assume that the earliest interpretation of Jesus (the one shot through and through with Jewish apocalyptic) is, because the earliest, an objective representation of the real intention of Jesus himself (p. 236). But what grounds have we for supposing that the latest interpretation, or any intermediate one, is nearer the truth? Dr Richardson answers: 'Only after several decades had gone by could the intention and work of Jesus be adequately assessed "in the perspective of history"' (p. 238). Very well: whose assessment is adequate and how do we judge it so? We are driven back to the Quest of the Historical Jesus after all, or, alternatively, to the authority of the Church (which Church?).

The latter seems to be the line taken by the dogmatic theologians to whom I have referred, and it is summed up by a Scottish Professor in New York as follows: 'The Gospels are kerygmatic documents proclaiming a faith in which the historical Jesus and the facts about him have undergone an irreversible metamorphosis into the Church's message.'[1] Professor MacQuarrie adds that 'history does not of itself settle the claim of Christianity. . . . Faith is primarily a matter for value-judgment, existential decision, faith-commitment, or however one may care to express it' (p. 150). Perhaps one may substitute for these long words 'leap in the dark'. Theologians who use language like this live in an atmosphere where a Gifford Lecturer or a simple layman cannot breathe.

Before I leave this wilderness I must refer to a scholarly and learned book by James M. Robinson: *A New Quest of the Historical Jesus* (London, 1961). He has read and considered all the works of Bultmann and his followers, and a vast amount of other literature as well. I have read his book twice, in a vain endeavour to understand his position, and I may therefore be meddling in matters beyond my competence. But I have felt it necessary not to overlook the case against me in the theology of the last generation.

[1] John MacQuarrie: *Studies in Christian Existentialism* (London, 1966), p. 140.

The key-words are *Kerygma*, encounter, eschatological, and existential. Why the first is not translated from the Greek I have not discovered. It means proclamation by a herald. In the passage where St Paul uses it, the Authorized Version translated it by 'preaching', and Luther by 'Predigt'. The New English Bible prefers 'gospel'. 'Proclamation' could surely serve.

We are told that 'Jesus can be encountered in the *Kerygma*; in this sense faith is not dependent on historiography, which as a matter of fact has been all but non-existent with regard to Jesus during most of the centuries of Christian faith' (p. 85). 'Historiography cannot and should not prove a *Kerygma* which proclaims Jesus as *eschatological* event calling for *existential* commitment' (p. 94). Hegel's terminology has been thought obscure, but it is crystal clear in comparison with the words here italicized by Mr Robinson and derived, I suppose, from existentialism.

He thinks that the nineteenth-century Quest failed because it rested on a positivistic view of history which is now outdated (this we have encountered before, e.g. in Dr Alan Richardson). We must accept instead 'the modern view of history. . . . The objectivity of modern historiography consists precisely in one's openness for the encounter, one's willingness to place one's intentions and views of existence in question, i.e. to learn something basically new about existence' (pp. 76–7). It might be possible to understand this if we had been given some examples of 'modern historiography'. R. G. Collingwood is quoted thrice in support of this view, but I cannot read him through Mr Robinson's eyes, or find this 'modern historiography' in his historical writings.[1]

When Mr Robinson says that when 'the historian's task was seen to consist in understanding those deep-lying intentions of the past, by involving one's selfhood in an encounter . . . then the *Kerygma* is formally analogous to this new approach to the historian's task' (p. 39), I can but express bewilderment. Nor am I enlightened when I am told (p. 59) that 'the original quest has been brought to an end by the rise of the *Kerygma* to the centre of twentieth-century theology'. His point here, I think, is that the historical Jesus cannot be isolated from the Christ of faith, and the original quest was wrong in so isolating him. But, we are told, it is equally important not to separate the Christ of faith from the

[1] Collingwood once said to me about Schweitzer's *Quest*, 'it has never been refuted'. If he had thought that it all rested on 'positivistic' history, he would have made short work of it.

historical Jesus (p. 78). Therefore a new quest of the historical Jesus is necessary, although it will be based on taking the Gospels, not as sources like Josephus or Tacitus, but as 'kerygmatized history' (p. 80). This quest is to be pursued, of course, in the light of 'modern historiography'. 'It is illegitimate to dodge the call of the *Kerygma* for existential faith in the saving event by an attempt to provide an objectively verified proof of its historicity' (p. 76). Apparently we are to begin by committing ourselves to the preaching or proclamation of Paul, and then to raise historical questions only in such a way that the answers will presuppose acceptance of this commitment. This is too tall an order for me, even if I assume that what these existentialist theologians are meaning is that the really important thing is not the bare facts recorded in the New Testament, but the 'encounter' and 'commitment' experienced afresh down all the generations. I would not wish to deny that there may be some truth in this, but I still have to ask: If the facts cannot be established, what are these theologians encountering?

Although, in an endeavour to be fair, I have dealt at disproportionate length with Mr Robinson, I cannot leave him without three further citations: (i) 'The original Disciples . . . had both their Easter faith and their factual memory of Jesus. They responded to this situation by intuitively explicating their memory until they found it in the *Kerygma*, i.e. by kerygmatizing their memory' (p. 86). I am not sure what 'intuitively explicating' means, but I wonder on what evidence Mr Robinson relies in so describing the response of the Disciples to their situation. (ii) A *curiosum* from Kierkegaard, quoted in a footnote (p. 75), I do not know whether with approval or not: 'If the contemporary generation had left nothing behind except . . . "We have believed that in such and such a year God showed himself in the puny form of a servant, taught and lived among us, and then died"—that would be more than enough.' Enough for what? For knowing what a generation in the first century AD believed, but not for giving us any reason for believing now. (iii) 'Man's quest for meaningful existence is his highest stimulus to scholarly inquiry' (p. 75). Such a stimulus has been denied to me. Is it because I was brought up to believe in God, and that therefore I have never had to embark on a quest for meaningful existence or to find myself in the gulf of meaninglessness beloved of some existentialists?

From the miasma of this wilderness it is a relief to turn to history once more. In 1949 T. W. Manson said: 'What is long overdue is a return to the study of the Gospels as historical documents concerning Jesus of Nazareth, rather than psychological case-material concerning the early Christians.'[1] Manson made some contributions himself to this study and he dealt faithfully, and to me convincingly, with the Form-Criticism which led to the historical scepticism which Manson repudiated. If he had lived, he would surely have welcomed a remarkable volume of essays called *Vindications* (London, 1966). The authors are concerned to combat the historical scepticism of the Form-Critics (first given currency in England, I think, by R. H. Lightfoot in his well-known Bampton Lectures), and to argue that the Gospels do provide evidence for the historical basis of Christianity. Here they follow Eduard Meyer, although they do not seem to mention him.

Professor R. P. C. Hanson of Nottingham points out that the Liberal Protestants wished to penetrate behind the Church's teaching to the real Jesus, and so to reconstruct orthodox dogmatics. The Form-Critics, on the other hand, as we have seen, start from the earliest preaching about Jesus, the proclamation of him as the risen Lord, and regard it as vital to emancipate Christian belief from the work of historians. Professor Hanson, accepting the original message, wants to give it a content. Curiosity about Jesus, the centre of the proclamation, is natural and proper, and he argues that it can be satisfied from a study of the Gospels. What is the use of a proclamation if the central figure of whom it speaks is a nose of wax or a void?

Professor Hanson goes on to contrast the procedures and presuppositions of the Form-Critics with those of practising historians concerned with the history of the early Roman Empire. When the available documentary evidence is considered, the contrast is extraordinary between the relative confidence of historians about the Emperor Tiberius and the radical scepticism of Form-Critics about Jesus. Professor Hanson's brother, a Professor at Hull, refers to the view that the New Testament writings are better evidence for the early Church's memory of Jesus than for any statement that they make about him, and his career. Suppose we apply this approach to the subject to other types of literature roughly contemporary with the New Testament. Consider the Life of Agricola by Tacitus. For our knowledge of Agricola we are almost wholly dependent on this book. It is obviously a work of *parti pris*; Tacitus venerated his father-in-law. Would any

[1] *Studies in the Gospels and Epistles* (Manchester, 1962), p. 8.

ancient historian say that we are better off with Tacitus's life than we could be if we had a few others, on the ground that what we find in *Agricola* is nothing about him, but only the living mind of Tacitus?

To summarize further the argument in these powerful essays would take us too far afield. But there is one point in Professor R. P. C. Hanson's essay which must be mentioned. 'Christian belief does not rest on historical evidence alone . . . but it is not totally emancipated from a consideration of historical evidence. . . . The Christ of the proclamation or the earliest preaching is meaningless if we refuse to regard any historical evidence about Christ as relevant. . . . Believers have always encountered Christ . . . through the activity of the Church. . . . The Christ who is believed is always the Risen Lord, the Christ worshipped in the Church. . . . It is therefore patently impossible that Christian belief in Christ could be wholly based on, or wholly demonstrated as true by, historical considerations alone' (pp. 66–7). If the word 'wholly' is emphasized, then this may be accepted, but it still leaves open a possibility which Professor Hanson does not consider. Even if history cannot prove his faith, might it not cast doubt on it, or at least on parts of it? The authors of *Vindications* do provide many arguments in favour of the view that their faith gains historical support from many passages in the Gospels, but may there not be something to say on the other side?

CHAPTER 9

WHAT IS IT REASONABLE TO BELIEVE?

It will have been observed that, in the course of my inquiry into what it is reasonable to believe, I have concentrated on history. Latterly a number of proponents of orthodox dogmatics, disliking what Schweitzer called the 'all too historical' Jesus, have treated the New Testament so radically that they have come to deny the possibility of discovering there (or anywhere) anything about Jesus himself, except that he died and was believed to have risen again. I have tried to argue that this jettisoning of nearly everything in the Gospels leaves the faith in the air.[1] I have been encouraged by some recent writers to depart from Loisy's views that the Gospels are not historical but liturgical or confessional, and from the not dissimilar view of some of those called Form-Critics. Therefore I return to what seems to me to be the crucial problem, that of the historicity of the Gospels. To evade it is to purchase orthodoxy at too high a price.

In my attack on this problem, my heroes have been Reimarus, Strauss, and Schweitzer. Those who today wish to return away from Form-Criticism to the historicity of the Gospels must reply, if they can, to these three men who were great writers as well as great historians. They all wrote in German, not the clearest or least verbose of languages; but they were masters of style, and their meaning is never in doubt. (I could not say the same about Barth and his *epigoni*.) They all raised questions which call for an answer, and it is not really surprising that those who shun the answers take refuge in dogmatics combined with radical scepticism about the Gospel record. I cannot find any answer which is compatible with orthodoxy, nor in this refuge can I find a home.

If you sit down 'in a cool hour' and read the New Testament through, you must be struck by extraordinary contrasts, for example, between the Synoptics and John, between the Gospels and the Epistles of St Paul (whether he wrote all of them or not). After a further reading, it is possible to find in John some leading ideas drawn from Judaism rather than from Greek philosophy, and in Paul some things implicit, if not explicit, in the Synoptics.

[1] In this view I have been fortified by Archbishop A. M. Ramsey's essay on *History and the Gospel* in *Studia Evangelica* IV, Berlin, 1968.

Paul is working with Judaic ideas which coincide with the Judaic apocalyptic found in the Synoptics also. But he is little interested in what Jesus himself taught; he mentions it seldom. This is a stone of stumbling.

Here I must refer to the work of Kirsopp Lake, whom I mentioned once before in Chapter 4. Forty-five years ago, when he lectured in Oxford, it was usual for Oxford theologians to pour scorn on his lectures and his conclusions, on the ground that his scholarship was only second-rate. It is true that he took but a second in Theology, but his real offence was that he was an Anglican clergyman who openly expressed disbelief in the creeds. A dispassionate reader is not likely to deny his scholarship (e.g. in *The Beginnings of Christianity*). Indeed, T. W. Manson, whose standing as a New Testament scholar no one is likely to dispute, described him in 1947 as 'one of the acutest and most learned New Testament scholars of our time.'[1]

I quote some things from Lake's Oxford lectures:[2]

'To the Protestant, adherence to truth means a willingness to learn, to confess ignorance and error, to accept new facts, and to follow the light: to a Catholic it means the acceptance of the unchangeable opinion of the Church speaking with the voice of God. Between these there can be no compromise and no peace' (p. 58). On this I comment that, if it be true, the number of Protestants would seem to have been diminishing.

'The faith of the creeds forms a consistent whole. It is not feasible to cut out the Virgin Birth but accept the Incarnation (which is far more difficult to believe), or to insist on the Trinity but cut out the Judgment to come. Those who framed the creeds meant what they said. They based themselves on an infallible Bible; they believed that Genesis was historical. Without the Creation and the Fall, Incarnation and Atonement are meaningless. The creeds can be proved, as the Thirty-nine Articles say, "by most certain warrant of Holy Scripture". The difficulty is that they cannot be proved by anything else. Proved by Scripture means taking Scripture as a whole and being content to find a proof *somewhere*. The Virgin Birth is "proved" because it is in Matthew and Luke; it does not matter that it is unknown to Mark or John or Paul. This sort of argument becomes impossible as soon

[1] *Studies in the Gospels and Epistles* (Manchester, 1962), p. 105. See also S. Neill, *op. cit.*, pp. 165–7.

[2] *The Religion of Yesterday and Tomorrow* (London, 1925).

as historical criticism gets to work on the books of the Bible' (pp. 79 ff.).

Admittedly, there is force in these contentions. As long ago as 1907 or 1908, N. P. Williams said that 'men are beginning to realize that in the future the choice will be between the whole of the historic faith and none of it'.[1] In February 1966 *The Times* printed an article headed *Hell in Eclipse—Threat to the whole Christian Faith.* Its anonymous author said: 'It should be difficult for Christians to believe that the chief doctrines upheld by the Church over centuries from its earliest formularies and creeds may now be convicted of gross error. The abandonment of one endangers the rest; they stand or fall together. When scriptural doctrines are discarded because of present unpopularity, a doubt is cast on the competence of the Holy Spirit to guide the Church in the past. Once that is done, the whole fabric of Christianity comes tumbling down.' Here Lake gains support from one whose position is otherwise the reverse of his. We are confronted with a choice between all or nothing. *Aut Caesar aut Nullus.* But I cannot believe that there is no escape between the horns of this dilemma.

Lake continues his dissent from orthodoxy: 'The Synoptics know nothing of Incarnation. They may be "adoptionist", i.e. they may teach that Jesus was adopted as Son of God, either at birth, or baptism, or Resurrection. Neither Jesus, nor those who first wrote his life, know anything of the central doctrine of Catholic theology. . . . How can the central doctrine be something which Jesus did not teach? He knew nothing of the Logos doctrine and never claimed to be God' (pp. 134–7). Here Lake is propounding again Lessing's distinction between the religion of Jesus and the religion which men have made out of him. This distinction carries little weight with theologians today, but with what historical justification?

There are instructive passages also in Lake's book on *St Paul* (London, 1934). He says that he does not believe that Jesus was God, and that St Paul did not either. 'I see no reason for believing about Jesus what he did not himself believe. . . . Jesus did not ask his followers to believe any special proposition about himself, but only to lead better lives' (p. 126). But what did Jesus believe about himself? Mark probably believed that Jesus was the Son of Man who would come at the end on the clouds of heaven (viii.

[1] E. W. Kemp: *N. P. Williams* (London, 1954), p. 12.

38, xiii. 26, xiv. 62), but Jesus does not say that he is.[1] He was a teacher, not a legislator (pp. 47–8), but he was convinced that he was an anointed messenger, commissioned to urge men to repent while there was still time, for the end was near (pp. 42–3).

What Paul did was to conflate the Davidic anointed one, who would restore the fortunes of Israel (i.e. in his view, all Christians) for a limited period before the end, with the anointed one who would come on the clouds of heaven at the end to judge the world. Hence Paul's belief that Jesus would reign over a community of Christians, raised with spiritual bodies, until the world ended. When Paul calls Jesus 'Lord', Kyrios, he is meaning that Jesus is the Jewish Messiah or anointed one. But 'Kyrios' in the Septuagint is the translation of 'Jehovah'. Thus, to Greek listeners, 'Kyrios' meant a divine being, like the heads of sacramental cults (pp. 121–3). Here, then, is the origin of Christianity and the prologue to the Fourth Gospel. Lake admits that I Corinthians viii. 6 presents difficulty, but he is not prepared to accept it as Pauline, any more than he will regard Ephesians and Colossians as Paul's. Perhaps this is kicking against the pricks of the contradictions and inconsistencies in the New Testament. It is hard to do so, but wrong to abandon in despair the attempt to get at historical truth.

Although Lake rejected most of the creeds, his attitude to them, and to the Anglican liturgy as a whole, reminds one of Loisy, who wanted to continue to celebrate Mass long after he had wandered away from orthodoxy. The creeds, Lake says, are part of the liturgy. 'The liturgical act of the services of the [Anglican] church, like the architectural art of its cathedrals, rouses a response in me which cannot be awakened by any modern service.' The creeds ought not to be altered in order to 'modernize' them, any more than it would be sensible to 'modernize' Durham Cathedral. The creeds ought to be rejected theologically and retained liturgically. The words 'I believe' mean that the author of the creed believed, not that the person who is repeating the creed believes. To many this will seem a strange attitude, and one difficult to

[1] Lake's view could be true only if 'Son of Man' were a title. But there is now abundant evidence to the contrary. In Daniel vii *Son of Man* means 'a man', i.e. in the context, Israel, and in the New Testament *Son of Man* is a surrogate for the first personal pronoun. In Matthew xi. 18–19, for example, Jesus is clearly referring to himself. See M. Black in *McCormick Quarterly*, May 1967, pp. 270–83, and especially the third edition of his *An Aramaic Approach to the Gospels and Acts* (Oxford, 1967), pp. 328–30.

sustain. But it will be understood by those who, not being Anglicans, are ever deeply moved by the language of the Prayer Book.

The lapse of forty-five years since Lake's lectures were delivered has produced a radical change in the theological outlook. The revival of orthodox dogmatics and the eclipse of liberalism give to Lake's work an archaic air, and some will be surprised that I have revived it. But his lectures made an indelible impression on the mind of an undergraduate, and to him they have never lost their freshness. It was then too that he first met Schweitzer, and it may not be surprising that he has never recovered from the impact of these two powerful personalities.

'It is impossible to write a life of Jesus; the materials for it do not exist.' I have read this assertion so often that I do not know where it originated. It may have been a reflection on the closing passage of Schweitzer's *Quest*. It may even go back to Strauss. Yet it is a judgment which cannot be accepted. If 'Life' is to mean the sort of biography in two or three or (Pusey) four or (Disraeli) six volumes, which was common before 1914, or the sort of psychological essay which has been commoner since then, or the biography which allows its subject to speak for himself in his letters and diaries, then it is true that in none of these manners can the life of Jesus be written. But if the Gospels do not provide biographical material, as some aver, then it is very difficult to understand the devotion of millions to Jesus the man. 'It is the name of Jesus, and not the name of Logos, that sounds sweet in the believer's ear.'[1]

The theologians who reject most of the Gospels as myth, or at least as not providing evidence for the life of Jesus, are apparently disciples of Paul, who was not interested in the life of Jesus, and of whom we know not more, and perhaps less, than we know about Jesus. Pauline Christology has conquered. It has dominated western civilization for nearly two thousand years. Now it does not dominate to the same extent. In 1922 I attended a service in the Roman Catholic Cathedral at Freiburg-im-Breisgau, and heard a sermon from the Archbishop. Much that he said I had too little German to understand, but again and again I heard the words '*Zurück zu Christus*' and they have been engraved on my mind ever since. It may be time to go back to the teaching of Jesus.

[1] Rev. L. B. Cross, in a letter to me.

What was he like? Barth, as we have seen, thinks that, if we stick to the Gospels, he is unimpressive compared with the founders of other religions, and even with some of the adherents of his own religion. But what was his own religion? It certainly was not Christianity.

A different impression of the personality of Jesus is provided in a short essay by K. Weidel:[1] 'Jesus stands before us as a Lord of men, with an unparalleled sovereignty of self-consciousness, the born commander to whose energy of will everything bows spontaneously, and yet a childlike heart, a friend of children. . . . With supreme piety to the Father and his law, he yet is the greatest revolutionary the world has ever known. Capable of passionate fury and wrath, a harsh judge . . . and, on the other hand, a man full of meekness and goodness, mild and forgiving, a friend of sinners. . . . Clear, peaceful, decisive, and conscious of his aim in his action, and then again passionately aroused, impulsive, beside himself, and standing under a higher compulsion. . . . King and beggar, hero and child, prophet and reformer, leader in battle and peace, master and servant . . . all this he was in his person. He could speak as seldom a man could, and he loved silence . . . He stands entirely by himself; in his appearance and his principles he was an absolute individualist, and yet he gave the impetus to a social brotherhood of mankind not yet after all this time achieved. . . . In a totally unusual strength of will-power there lies the centre of his personality. Only a really mighty self-mastery could bear such a multiplicity of contrary dispositions and motives without damage, and unify them into a compact general effect.'[2]

Here at least there is what seems to me to be a necessary admission, and it is a pity that Weidel's work is not better known. Jesus was a tremendous personality, totally unlike anyone that the Disciples had ever encountered. It is true that the opposition of the Pharisees shows that they took him seriously, but he did not

[1] Quoted here from Schweitzer: *Geschichte*, etc., edn. cit., pp. 580–2.

[2] These opposed characteristics in the personality of Jesus are well pointed out in a remarkable essay by Karl Jaspers, to which Professor Matthew Black drew my attention. See *Die Auffassung der Persönlichkeit Jesu* in *Essays Presented to Leo Baeck* (London, 1954), pp. 36–49. Jaspers says it is easy to say what Jesus was not, e.g. that he was not the founder of a Church, but to say what he was is more difficult. Jaspers proceeds to deal with what Jesus was as a person, with his place in the history of his time, and with the essence of his teaching. The last section emphasizes the connection of Jesus with Judaism. The essay commands my assent almost throughout, and I wish that it was more generally accessible.

convince educated Jewry, and we may well wonder why. This is one of the chief historical problems, and I have too little knowledge of Judaism to attempt a solution.

Somehow the beginning and the spread of Christianity must be explained. After the Crucifixion the Disciples all forsook him and fled. Shortly afterwards they are filled with new confidence. They were convinced that their Master was indeed the Messiah, the Son of God, who would shortly return and place them on thrones in his Kingdom.

Hegel told us that to consider the Resurrection as an event has nothing to do with religion. Bultmann today says much the same. This, however, is an evasion. The contradictions which Reimarus found in the Gospel narratives of the Resurrection and the post-Resurrection appearances cannot be gainsaid.[1] But there were communities of Jewish Christians, not only in Jerusalem, but in many Near Eastern cities, and even in Rome, before our Gospels were written. What could that event have been which gave confidence to the Disciples, and provided them with a message which convinced so many others? They were Jews: fanatical monotheists, and yet they worship Jesus as the Risen Lord; sabbatarians, and they give up the Sabbath and assemble instead on the Lord's Day; believing that crucifixion meant that the crucified one was abandoned by God, and yet so quickly believing, in this instance, the reverse. What was it that produced this sudden *bouleversement* of the Jewish faith?[2]

The questions invite the answer: the Resurrection. But suppose we ignore Hegel and ask whether this was an historical event. The most recent answer which I have seen is that of Professor Lampe of Cambridge.[3] He points out that the conversion of St

[1] It is only a few that have been removed by a study of the Aramaic background of the Gospels. See M. Black, *op. cit.*, pp. 136–8.

[2] The questions come from Sir T. M. Taylor's sermon on The Coming One in *Where one man stands* (Edinburgh, 1960). E. Meyer, *op. cit.* (iii, p. 243), says that the early Christians did continue to keep the Sabbath, and I have read this in some more recent work.

[3] G. W. H. Lampe and D. M. MacKinnon: *The Resurrection* (London, 1966). He had at least three predecessors: (i) Kirsopp Lake: *The Resurrection of Jesus Christ* (London, 1907), pp. 35 ff., 265 ff. At pp. 251–2 he adds the interesting suggestion that the women went to the wrong tomb. There was plenty of rock tombs in the area. Speculation has no end. (ii) L. B. Cross: *Jesus, his Resurrection and Ascension* in *The Modern Churchman* (September, 1946): 'In so far as Paul describes the appearance of the Risen Messiah [to the Apostles] in exactly the same language as he describes the appearance to himself, we may safely conclude that he did not think that their experience differed in any way from his

Paul was the result of a vision specially vouchsafed to him, although in one place we are told that those with him heard the voice, and in another that they did not (Acts ix. 7, xxii. 9). Paul seems to regard his experience of the Risen Lord as similar to the experiences of all the others whom he mentions. He says nothing about an empty tomb and presumably had never heard of it. All that he says about *our* being raised, including his analogy of the grain dying, is against a belief in the resurrection of the *body*. The stories about the empty tomb are due to reflection on what the visions of the Risen Lord implied. Bodily corruption is something from which Jesus, as man, could not be exempt. The empty tomb is suggestive of a Docetic Christ, one who did not fully share the lot of man.

This is not without plausibility.[1] If, when Paul was persecuting the Jewish Christians and had heard from them, directly or indirectly, stories of the empty tomb, and surely he must have done if the stories were then current, it is strange that he makes no mention of them.

Plausibility is not proof, and in this matter proof is impossible. The historian is faced with contradictory evidence; he may construe it as he will. But the one thing he cannot do is to deny that something tremendous happened, for otherwise the origin of Christianity is inexplicable.

It is perhaps important to point out that it was not simply a resurrection that revolutionized the lives of the Disciples. The Gospels, let alone the Old Testament, provide other stories about persons raised from the dead, and from them no new religion resulted. See, for example, the strange (and incredible) passage in Matthew xxvii. 52–3. The point was that it was Jesus, this towering personality, who had risen from the dead. This it was which convinced the Disciples and confirmed their expectation of the new age. Their Lord and Master was with them yet, the Messiah indeed, preparing the twelve thrones on which they were to sit (Matthew xix. 28). The inferences drawn from the belief in the Resurrection are more difficult to believe than the belief itself.

St Paul did not know Jesus 'after the flesh'.[2] His conviction of

own. He cannot have thought in terms of physical appearance as he certainly did not believe in any empty tomb.' (iii) Joel Carmichael: *The Death of Jesus* (Penguin Books, 1966), pp. 168–70. (This was first published in 1963.)

[1] Bishop S. Neill (*op. cit.*, p. 287 fn.) says that Paul 'recognizes that his own encounter with the Risen Christ was different from that of the other Apostles', but he quotes no evidence.

[2] Whatever the words *κατὰ σάρκα* may mean.

a revelation, granted to himself, turned him away from persecuting the Christians, and made him believe that Jesus was the Messiah. Full himself of the messianic hopes of Judaism and its apocalyptic, he preached the Risen Lord who, he hoped, would return on the clouds of heaven in his own lifetime. Moreover, he is confident that 'because he lives, we shall live also'. On what is his confidence based? Can it be shared today? To both questions my answer is: I do not know.

Some at least of the teaching of Jesus was equally rooted in Judaism. He is reported to have said 'If they hear not Moses and the Prophets, neither will they be persuaded though one rose from the dead' (Luke xvi. 31). He came to fulfil and not to abolish the law.

The message of the Apostles seems to have spread with great rapidity to Asia Minor, Greece, and Rome, presumably to communities of Jews, at least at first. It was apparently Paul who first clearly reinterpreted the Gospel as applicable to Gentiles also. His message was still rooted in Judaism, because it is unintelligible apart from the Old Testament. When he was preaching, the New Testament did not exist. He went first to the synagogues to proclaim that justification was by faith in the atoning death of Jesus, the Messiah, and not by adherence to the law; and yet, except in relation to circumcision and certain food regulations, which had little reference to conduct, the law remained. This is why the early Jewish Christians were essentially a Judaic sect. But Paul preached salvation to the Gentiles and this was 'what the masses wanted—deliverance from the misery of this world, from the rule of evil powers, demons, and the devil, and instead a hope of a happy life beyond, an elevation into the heavenly sphere of the divine'.[1] Thus did Paul begin to make an impact on Gentiles as well as Jews.

At some stage, however, perhaps when the author of the Fourth Gospel propounded the Logos doctrine, of which Paul was ignorant, the Christian faith became something different from that of a Jewish sect. How could it have found acceptance so quickly and so far afield if it had not chimed in with, or explained, or elaborated, other faiths already current in southern Europe and the Near East?[2] These early Christian communities would seem to have been as indifferent to, or as ignorant of, the teaching of Jesus as

[1] E. Meyer, *op. cit.*, iii, p. 399.

[2] This was worked out by W. Bousset (my father's teacher in Göttingen). See *Kyrios Christos* (1913) and S. Neill, *op. cit.*, pp. 164–5.

Paul was himself. If, as now seems to me to be incontestable, the Synoptic Gospels provide good historical evidence for the life and teaching of Jesus, then it is clear that he did not teach a great deal of what the Apostles, Nicene, and Athanasian creeds so confidently affirm. Is it not a bold affirmation that his actual teaching is irrelevant to a faith which it is reasonable to accept? May it not be that Lessing was right to point out, in the short note which I quoted in Chapter 3, that the religion of Jesus we know from the Gospels, while the Christian religion is a different matter?

But it is not merely a matter of what we can know from the Gospels. The question is: How much of what we know can we accept? Jesus came not to destroy the law but to fulfil it. Yet there is also the statement that the law and the Prophets were until John (Luke xvi. 16). Paul abrogates the law; it is not to be binding on the Gentiles. If thus far we accept Paul, we may be left with the Prophets, and there is no denying the religious insight in much of their writings. The same is true of the Wisdom literature. 'The spirit of man is the candle of the Lord' (a favourite quotation) comes from Proverbs (xx. 27). But we have to pick and choose, not only in the Prophets, the Wisdom books, and the Psalms, but in the reported teaching of Jesus himself. The end of the world, prophesied for the first century AD, has not yet happened. We cannot any longer accept Jewish apocalyptic. Schweitzer at one time refused to pick and choose between the moral and religious teaching recorded in the Synoptics; but Harnack insisted on discarding the husk and retaining the kernel. The husk was the eschatological and apocalyptic teaching, while the kernel was the insistence, in morality, on motive. It is hard not to sympathize.

The difficulty with Schweitzer is to explain the spread of the Christian religion beyond the bounds of Jewry. The difficulty with Harnack is that liberal Christians, when they came to distinguish husk from kernel, had such diverse views about what the kernel really was; scarcely anything was left that no one rejected. Nevertheless, this is the real historical difficulty still. Christianity, unlike its contemporaries, such as the mystery religions and Gnosticism, had, as I have said so often, an historical foundation. But even if that foundation can be ascertained, and the story of Christian origins satisfactorily settled, the question would still arise of how much we can reasonably believe today.

It seems to me that Reimarus, Strauss, and Schweitzer provide overwhelming evidence for the view that apocalyptic was one central element in the teaching of Jesus, and this belongs to a bygone age. But this does not end the matter. His teaching contained elements which burst the bonds of Judaism, and provided a potentially universal message about the nature of God and his Kingdom, about man's relation to him, and about man's proper manner of life. According to this message, God is to be worshipped as a loving Heavenly Father, who is ready to forgive the penitent sinner, while man must rise above righteousness and law to sincerity and truth, basing his conduct on love of God and his neighbour. If to have a religion is reasonable at all, then faith in this one is reasonable. Of course, it cannot be proved, but it chimes in with the highest reaches of man's mind and spirit. It will be observed, however, that, thus stated, this religion cannot believe in Hell, or eternal torment, and it has no need of a mediator or of an atonement, both of which spring from Old Testament ideas. The same disbelief is true of Covenant, whether old or new. How could there be a Covenant with God? A mediator is needed only if God is conceived, as by the Jews, as wholly transcendent. But Jesus is a mediator, in the sense that he taught a doctrine, transcending Judaism, about God, men's conduct, and the Holy Spirit. In this sense it is true that 'no man cometh to the Father but by me' (John xiv. 6).

This distinction between the religion of Jesus and Christianity, on which I have laid so much emphasis, was graphically outlined long ago by Jowett in one of his College Sermons:[1] If Jesus came back to earth he would teach 'purity of thought as well as of word and act, the not doing of things that we may be seen of men . . ., the seeking first the Kingdom of God, the forgiveness of injuries . . . "that we may be children of our Father which is in Heaven". What [you say] only the Sermon on the Mount! We thought he would speak to us of apostolical succession, of baptismal regeneration, of justification by faith only, of final assurance, of satisfaction and atonement. . . . We thought that we should have been confirmed in those points of faith or practice in which we differ from others, and that they would have been condemned . . ., that he would have decided authoritatively disputed points, saying "thus and thus shall he think who would be saved". But he just puts us off with parables. . . . The language of theology seems never to fall from his lips, but only "Thou shalt love the Lord thy God, and thy neigh-

[1] *Selected Passages from the Theological Writings of B. Jowett* (London, 1902), pp. 14–16.

bour as thyself".' It is not surprising that Jowett was persecuted by Tractarians and Evangelicals alike, but it is easier to persecute than to answer.

An answer there is. The creeds and the whole apparatus of dogmatic theology represent the intellectual labour of centuries, the Church's endeavour, under the guidance of the Holy Spirit, it has believed, to state and develop in detail the implications of the Christian faith as it was originally preached by the Apostles, especially Paul. If ever man's reason was rigorously employed, it was employed on this task. 'Rationalism' during the last century has generally meant an attack on, or at least a negative attitude to, religion in general and the Christian religion in particular. But the implication that the history of doctrine or of theology is a history of the irrational is patently false. From Anselm (to go no earlier) to Barth (to come no later), rigorous logic and acuteness of intellect have gone to the making of theology. The trouble is that this whole enterprise rested on certain fundamental presuppositions, and the foundations are crumbling. It may be something like what has happened in the history of mathematics, when the presuppositions of Euclid are questioned.

Nevertheless, this is only part of the answer to which I have referred. The other part is that the Church was founded on a rock and was promised the guidance of the Holy Spirit. It therefore has authority, at least in matters of faith and doctrine. Why not accept that authority in religion, just as you accept the findings of experts in other fields? Apart from the fact that the extent to which we accept these findings nowadays is limited to elementary matters, because we know how widely experts differ on the frontiers of knowledge, the question is: *Whose* authority in religion are we to accept? We must use our reason or our intelligence in choosing an authority, and can we put our reason or our intelligence to sleep thereafter? Is it never to examine what authority dictates? If reason is to abdicate in this way, then the only authority which it can reasonably accept is the only one which claims infallibility. If briefed to defend such an acceptance, I would have to return the brief.

Professor Hodges offers us a fresh alternative:[1] 'There is hardly a better safeguard against coming to believe in Christianity than to begin by regarding it . . . as a plurality of propositions or articles of belief, each of which can and must be considered . . . separately.

[1] In *Journal of Theological Studies*, October 1966.

For each there must be detailed evidences . . . and it is an offence against intellectual integrity for anyone to profess to believe more than he can in this way see for himself.' What is required instead is a 'global vision and a global acceptance . . . an intuitive grasp of the Faith as a whole' (p. 536). 'Wherever the vision is genuinely seen, it is authoritative and carries conviction' (p. 538). 'No one,' Professor Hodges adds, quoting von Balthasar, 'no one can reject Christ if he has really and truly seen him' (p. 534). I comment: To ask for a 'global vision' of the Catholic Faith, as if it were a picture and not a series of statements, is too tall an order for me. As for 'really seeing', this can but mean that it is only believers who 'really see'. Seeing is believing. Or, in the words of the hymn: 'Only believe, and thou shalt see'. Only.

In approaching the close of these reflections I will take a short look backward over the route that we have travelled, in order to see how far the questions that I have posed have been answered. Many of my conclusions have been negative. For example, I have explicitly rejected as unhistorical the view of Reimarus and Kant and, at one time, Hegel, that what Jesus taught was no more than natural religion and rational morality. I have also found no reason for belief in the verbal inspiration of the Scriptures. I have been unable to share either the radical scepticism of so many modern theologians about the historicity of the Gospels, or the view of Hegel and others that history does not matter, and that theology, and the Christian faith can be indifferent to it. Strauss's endeavour to restore dogmatically what he had destroyed critically is inevitably a failure.

Several times I have stressed Lessing's distinction between the religion of Jesus and Christianity. The historian cannot but accept this distinction, and I have described as a reasonable faith certain *parts* of the teaching of Jesus. Like Harnack, I distinguish between husk and kernel, but what is the basis of this distinction? Schweitzer at one time thought that we could not pick and choose, but he did later suggest that a criterion of selection might be found in philosophy. This, I think, is sound so far as it goes. A man's religion is not something to be kept in a watertight compartment, away from the rest of a man's intellectual, aesthetic, and moral life. In some people it may become so dominant as to be not a partner of their other experiences, but a ruler over them. Religious mania exists. Normally, however, religious, moral, philosophical, and other beliefs will react on each other. It cannot therefore be surprising if, after nearly two thousand years of history, we must reject some things in the Scriptures. If Jesus was, as orthodoxy has always claimed, a man, sharing to the full the human lot, he did not walk on the waves or still a storm. Jewish beliefs about angels and demons, which Paul certainly shared, find no place within our cosmogony. Heaven is not a place above the clouds. The Ascension is therefore incredible. So I must, in candour, report, but others think differently.

Since in my philosophy I have learnt so much from Hegel, it is natural that I should find help from him in my religious studies too. Although I rejected his general conception of religion as a metaphor which philosophy can translate, there is much in the teaching summarized above in Chapters 4 and 5 that I accept.

Although the teaching of Jesus was rooted in Judaism and was often expressed as if it were for the Jews only, it contained elements which burst the bonds of Judaism, and were fundamentally opposed to its spirit. Here Hegel's essay on the *Spirit of Christianity* must be right. Otherwise how could it have happened that Christianity spread so rapidly through Asia Minor and to Western Europe? The answer may be that the Christian missionaries did not preach what Jesus taught, but only a new religion about him. This seems to me to be true.

The leaders of the Jews did not believe that he was the Messiah. He did not appear to them after the Resurrection. Some say that if the tomb had not been empty, the opponents of the Disciples could have confounded them by producing the body of Jesus. Well, why did they not? Was it because the Disciples were not claiming an empty tomb, but an experience of a risen Lord who appeared amongst them when the doors were shut and who vanished before the eys of the travellers to Emmaus? If so, then the address to Thomas and the eating of bread and fish cannot be authentic.

I return to Hegel: 'Everything high, noble, good in man is divine; it comes from God and is his spirit'. Here is the essential doctrine that God is not just transcendent, *Deus absconditus*, but somehow also immanent in man as his spirit. This protest against a purely transcendent and distant God has been echoed in our time by a book which I have mentioned already—*Honest to God* by J. A. T. Robinson. The protest must be accepted, however difficult it may be to assimilate the obscure proclamations of Bonhoeffer which have captivated the Bishop. The doctrine of the Holy Spirit has perhaps been the most neglected of all the clauses in the Creed. But it is essential for anyone who regards man as not just natural but as having a foot in another realm altogether, the supra-natural or spiritual realm. It is easier to believe in the Third Person of the Trinity than the Second.[1]

No one, so far as I know, has emphasized and expounded the doctrine of the Spirit as Hegel has. Of course, it is very difficult to ascertain what this doctrine meant at the beginning of Christianity, and especially what the gift of the Spirit was at Pentecost, or was regarded as being then. Man's consciousness of finitude, Hegel holds, is already a consciousness of the infinite, and a consciousness that the finite has its real being in the infinite. And this is religion.

Christianity has taught that there is a real union of infinite and finite spirit. The difficulty is to hold fast to the difference and yet the unity of the two. Here at its most extreme is Hegel's doctrine of the unity of opposites. It is easy to grasp this unity in the concavity and convexity of a curve, but it is far more difficult when we rise above what can be seen, or above nature, to the spiritual life. And yet the life of man, in its self-transcendence, witnesses to this unity. The diremption between what we are and what we should be is something of which we are conscious, and we would not strive to be better, to live a more spiritual life, if the spirit did not dwell in us. The consciousness of man as spirit is somehow a one-ness with Spirit itself, a one-ness of man and God, if only man could raise himself always to the spiritual level. This is what Jesus did, if we may use the Gospels as containing history. This is where philosophy works in with religion, just as I have claimed (in my book, *Action*) that moral experience does too.

What, after the historical inquiry which has been the subject of the preceding chapters, is to be said of Jesus of Nazareth? I have already made it plain that no account of him, like Barth's, which belittles the personality can be given any historical credit. A candid reader of the Gospels must find there, whatever he may reject as myth or disbelieve as Judaic apocalyptic, an overpowering personality. As Sir T. M. Taylor said, occasions are reported when people were afraid of him, 'and they had every reason to be'.[2] Whatever you may discard as dated, there still remains what challenges, even after two millennia.

[1] In Chapter 10 I have elaborated, and sometimes repeated what I say here.
[2] *op. cit.*, p. 66.

Nevertheless, when we consider the orthodox doctrine of the Incarnation, we must draw attention to some passages in the Gospels. As others have said, it is those passages which create the greatest difficulties for orthodoxy that are most likely to be authentic. First, why callest thou me good? None is good save God only. No one knows the hour, not I, but the Father only. These statements are not compatible with the doctrine of the Second Person of the Trinity. Secondly, the cries of agony from the Cross. God had forsaken him. His project had failed. What project? Here there is room for doubt. What was betrayed? Why was he crucified? Did he preach a Kingdom which was to deliver Israel, as the travellers on the road to Emmaus thought, or a Kingdom which was really meant not to be of this world, but in or amongst you? Did he use the language of his day, as he had to do, although he meant really to upset Jewry, as Hegel suggested? What was his connection with Zealots and Essenes and Qumran?

To these questions there are answers in some comparatively recent books which have interested me, even if they are not always convincing. If we put to the average church member the question who was responsible for the death of Jesus, and why, we might well be told that he was condemned to death by the leaders of the Jews, the Sanhedrin, for blasphemy. Since they had no power to execute the sentence, they handed him over to Pilate on a political charge. Pilate thought him innocent, but, under duress and with great reluctance, had him scourged and crucified. The Jews accepted responsibility for his execution.

But this is all very dubious. The picture painted by the Evangelists of Pilate's conduct of the trial of Jesus contradicts all that we know of him from other sources. He seems to have been cruel and merciless, and Luke may hint at the truth when he mentions 'the Galileans whose blood Pilate had mingled with their sacrifices' (xiii. 1).

An eminent Roman historian, A. N. Sherwin-White, defends[1] the authenticity of most of the Gospel records of the trial of Jesus, as well as of the trials of Paul in Acts. He rejects—(as usual, there is always something to reject)—the time-table in Luke, because it places the reference to Pilate too late in the day. The Roman Procurator's working day ended at mid-day. The Sanhedrin knew this, and therefore, to avoid encroaching on the Passover, it had to meet hurriedly at night. Mr Sherwin-White is quite sure that

[1] *Roman Society and Roman Law in the New Testament* (Oxford, 1963).

the Sanhedrin did not have the power to inflict capital punishment, except on pagan trespassers in the Temple: the stoning of Stephen, and the projected stoning of the woman taken in sin, were lynchings, or cases of exceeding authority, paralleled by others in the Empire. What Mr Sherwin-White has shown is that there is no reason to doubt a nocturnal trial before the Sanhedrin, and that the recorded procedure before Pilate accords with what is known about Roman legal procedure in the Empire, just as he has shown that the author of Acts reports correctly Roman administrative procedure in the Near East in the first century AD. It was altered later.

But difficulties remain. Was Jesus guilty of the charge on which he was condemned by Pilate? Mr Sherwin-White ascribes Pilate's hesitation to the fact that Jesus had not answered his accusers. He does not dispute the contention of Professor Brandon: 'The most certain thing known about Jesus of Nazareth is that he was crucified by the Romans as a rebel against their government in Judaea'.[1] But was he guilty? Before coming to Professor Brandon's book, it is worth while to look at three others.

(i) Robert Eisler's *The Messiah Jesus and John the Baptist* (London, 1931) is not recent, but it is a fascinating and learned book, though it has found favour with few New Testament scholars, and I admit that I have not been convinced. He relies to a large extent on a Slavonic translation of Josephus, but, although this seems to be conclusive against Drews (if any other than Schweitzer's refutation of Drews is required), it is a subjective insight, as a rule, which finds interpolations in Josephus and the New Testament, made by Christian scribes in the days before printing (are all the scribes supposed to be writing in the same place?) The possibility of these cannot be denied, but all Eisler's ingenuity fails to make plausible his argument that all that is said of the baptism of Jesus was really said of the Baptist, and that the temptations were temptations of John.

However, there may be more force in his contention that the Crucifixion was a political act of the first importance, because the carpenter had been hailed as the liberator of Israel, and as Saviour King, at a time when Jerusalem was full of pilgrims.

There is also an interesting suggestion about interpolations in the text of Josephus in relation to the judgment of Pilate:

'Pilate . . . had that wonder-worker brought up, and after he

[1] S. G. F. Brandon: *Jesus and the Zealots* (Manchester, 1967), p. 1.

had held an inquiry concerning him, he pronounced this judgment. He is [a benefactor but not] a malefactor [nor] a rebel [nor] covetous of kingship.' If the words bracketed are regarded as an interpolation designed to put the blame on the Jews, then the judgment of Pilate becomes intelligible and consistent with everything else known of him. This is a very tempting conjecture.

(ii) Paul Winter[1] begins by accepting the view that the Gospels were not written to guide historians. The tradition which reached the Evangelists was already an interpreted tradition. Nevertheless, it is possible to discern the truth, especially that responsibility for the Crucifixion was Roman and not Jewish. Jesus was no Zealot. He preached the Kingdom of God which comes without observation, not the coming of his own kingdom. But once he was regarded as the Messiah, the Disciples, and the people generally, were bound to think of him as David's son who would restore the throne of his ancestors, expel the Romans, and introduce a paradisal age of peace for Israel. Consequently, the Sanhedrin, which had a political as well as a legal jurisdiction, feared that his preaching might lead to an insurrection, and therefore delated him to Pilate.

The Procurator sent a Roman Cohort (John xviii) to arrest him on a charge of rebellion (Mark xiv, John xviii). He was conducted to a local Jewish administrative authority the same night (Mark, Luke, John). Next morning, after a brief deliberation by the Jewish authorities, he was handed back to the Romans for trial (Mark, Luke, John). Pilate sentences him to death by crucifixion (Mark, Tacitus), and the sentence was carried out in accordance with Roman penal procedure.

Although Winter admits that Jesus had friendly relations with revolutionaries, and chose a Zealot as a disciple, he shares Meyer's belief that Jesus was not guilty. Attempts to exonerate Pilate and throw the blame on the Jews were attempts to evade Roman persecution of the Christians. Winter argues carefully and dispasionately, but Sherwin-White thinks him mistaken on some points of Roman law, and, on the question of guilt or innocence, Carmichael and Brandon, as we shall see, make points against Winter's conclusion.

(iii) Joel Carmichael[2] argues that Jesus was guilty of the charge. He was a rebel. He was the herald of the Kingdom of God and

[1] *On the Trial of Jesus* (Berlin, 1961).
[2] *The Death of Jesus* (Penguin Books, 1966).

tried to take it by storm. We can dimly discern the outlines of a visionary who was also a man of action, and who attempted to set in motion the machinery of God's will. In support of this contention, Carmichael appeals to the ceremonial entry into Jerusalem, with its welcoming crowds. Without a large number of followers he could not have occupied the Temple and overturned the tables of the money-changers. The truth of this is obvious when the vast size of the Temple and the multitude of people in it are visualized. This in fact may have been the insurrection referred to in Mark xv. 7. Carmichael also supports his argument by citing the passages where Jesus refers to taking the sword. The result is a somewhat one-sided picture of Jesus of Nazareth, but the book fascinates by its ingenuity and fairness. It concludes by offering an explanation, which I find plausible, of how Christianity, a new religion altogether, arose and spread.

It is time to turn to the important work of Professor S. G. F. Brandon. He has a great admiration for Robert Eisler and there is a similarity between their writings. Both do not hesitate to make bold conjectures, but I have found Brandon the more convincing of the two. I confine myself to his magisterial book, *Jesus and the Zealots* (Manchester, 1967), but *The Fall of Jerusalem and the Christian Church* (1951) and *Man and his Destiny in the Great Religions* (1962) have the same high qualities and should not be neglected by any student of Christian origins.

Brandon agrees with Carmichael about the triumphal entry and the cleansing of the Temple. This latter must have been a riot or 'insurrection', and the Roman garrison in the Antonia (a fort overlooking the Temple) must have seen it. Whatever the attitude of the Pharisees and the Sanhedrin, the Zealots were revolutionaries. They were associated with Galilee, and Jesus chose one of them as a disciple. If a Communist were converted to the Roman Catholic Church, would he still be known as 'Simon the Communist'?

Consequently, Brandon agrees again with Carmichael, against Winter, that Jesus was guilty of the political charge laid against him.

How is it, then, that the Gospels exonerate Pilate and put the blame on the Jews? Brandon's answer is that Mark, the earliest surviving Gospel, was written in Rome shortly after AD 70 in order to save Jewish Christians from the charge of being anti-Roman. He makes a powerful case. He has failed to convince a reviewer (*T.L.S.*, April 27, 1967), who cannot believe that Mark was written to prove the exact opposite of what Jewish Christians in Rome knew to be the truth. But Brandon can point to Acts v. 28, where the Sanhedrin accuse Peter of 'intending to bring this man's blood upon us'. Presumably the Sanhedrin knew the truth, i.e. that responsibility for the execution was Roman.

Brandon makes a strong case for believing that Mark was written to disassociate Jesus and the Disciples from the nationalist movement which was crushed in AD 70, and to introduce some Pauline universalism. Mark quotes Aramaic words six times, and translates five of them. Why did he not translate 'Cananaean'? The word is Aramaic for 'Zealot'. This is surely significant (one of Brandon's favourite words).

The teaching of Jesus was tied up with Judaic Messianism, but with some modifications. He may have tried to spiritualize the conception (see Mark viii. 33). When the Disciples believed in the Resurrection, they also believed in the imminence of the Second Coming. They remained in Jerusalem and were to all appearance simply another Jewish sect.

Paul, however, claimed to have a direct revelation of Jesus, possibly as a pre-existent being, the Lord of Glory. He cares nothing for the life of Jesus, but builds a soteriology on his death for all mankind. This brings him into conflict with the Jerusalem Church. The conflict is played down in Acts, but it is obvious in the Epistles. Acts, though a glorification of Paul, is also something of an eirenicon. By the time it was written, the Jerusalem Church had been destroyed, and old controversies had died away.

Matthew was written in Alexandria and was addressed to the remnant of the Jerusalem Church there. There are anti-Pauline hints in it. This is not surprising if the Alexandrian Church was founded by Peter. Why did Paul never go to Alexandria? Was Alexandria not probably the 'other place' to which Peter went (Acts xii. 17)?[1] It had a very large Jewish population, and Judaic relations with Egypt were old enough.

It is not possible within a short compass to do justice to Brandon's book. But alike in style, learning, acuteness, and insight, it deserves to stand on the shelf with the great Germans of the past.

[1] E. Meyer, *op. cit.*, iii, p. 421, suggests Lydda, Joppa, or Caesarea, but gives no reason. T. W. Manson, *op. cit.*, Ch. 3, refers to the association of Mark with Peter, and to the tradition that Mark founded the Church of Alexandria, but perhaps as an offshoot of the Church of Rome. This seems very improbable. Brandon is more convincing here.

As a contribution to a new quest of the historical Jesus, it is worth far more than Mr Robinson and all his Bultmannian friends together. No doubt Brandon is too speculative, too fond of the argument from silence, but I think that, on most of the points summarized here, he has established his case, and his account of the Zealots and their activities is surely of permanent value.

Meanwhile, after this long excursus, I return to the quotations which suggest that, although Jesus depended upon God and did his will more faithfully than anyone, so far as we know, has done since, he was far from claiming equality with God himself. I add one other. How did he teach us to pray? His prayer does not conclude, as most Christian prayers do, with a petition to be heard 'for Christ's sake'.

It will be urged that all this is not to the purpose, because the pathway of natural religion, whether philosophical or historical, leads in the wrong direction. John Calvin said (but was not the first to say) that outside the bosom of the Church there could be no hope of the remission of sins or of salvation.[1] The Pope would have said the same, even if his conception of the Church was not quite the same as Calvin's. What has happened in the last century, according to the late Dean of Chichester, is the 'rediscovery of the fact that the foundation of one Holy Catholic and Apostolic Church by Jesus Christ is as much a truth of revelation as the doctrine of the Incarnation itself'.[2] Perhaps it would be safer to substitute the word 'belief' for the word 'fact', but it is doubtless the spread of this belief which has done so much today to promote the oecumenical movement. If this belief could be adopted, then these historical inquiries might well become as 'cold and strain'd and ridiculous' as Hume's investigations into human nature. But whatever the word ἐκκλησία may mean in the New Testament, it certainly does not have the associations of the word 'church' today.[3] If, therefore, the foundation of one Holy Catholic Church by Jesus Christ is a truth of revelation, it is, equally with the Bodily Assumption of the Virgin Mary, unverifiable by historical investigation, and equally one which I am unable to find reasons for believing. The first verse of the well-known hymn, 'The

[1] Quoted by Very Rev. A. S. Duncan Jones in *Northern Catholicism, edn. cit.*, pp. 446–7.

[2] *ibid.*, p. 446.

[3] Hoskyns and Davey in *The Riddle of the New Testament* (London, 1958) try to prove the contrary, but it seems to me that the evidence they quote disproves their own contention.

Church's one Foundation', is almost an epitome of what I disbelieve.

It may be thought that the result of my picking and choosing is negative (which to a large extent it is) and mistaken. The same criticism was urged against Schweitzer, only to provoke Burkitt's famous remark: 'Mistake or no mistake, it drove Schweitzer out to Africa as a medical missionary'. To such heroism I cannot aspire. It seems to me, however, that, even after the apocalyptic is stripped away along with the prudential morality in parts of Matthew, and along with myth like the Virgin Birth, nature miracles, and the Ascension, enough is left to make Jesus the religious and moral teacher of our civilization. He taught as one having authority and not as the Scribes. He has still the authority of the truth which we recognize as truth when we encounter it, harmonizing and explaining the higher realms of our experience. It may thus not be unreasonable to adopt some lines from J. G. Whittier's great hymn:

> O Lord and Master of us all . . .
> What may thy service be?
> Nor name nor form nor ritual word
> But simply following thee.

What it is reasonable for a man to believe depends on the man that he is and on the experience that he has had. Consequently, others situated differently from me will find it reasonable to believe much more than I can. They may be better historians than I am. My conviction, however, is that history (along with philosophy) will have the last word, whether in support of orthodox dogmatics or not.

It may seem odd that I should say that what it is reasonable to believe varies with the man and his experience. Surely the reasoning which proves the theorem of Pythagoras is the same for every man, no matter what his experience, training, knowledge, or character? But I am asking what it is reasonable to *believe*. I am not talking about proof. Belief there must be when reasoning ends. What it is reasonable to believe depends on weighing evidence. Sometimes the evidence is overwhelming, as, for instance, against a belief in biblical inerrancy. But often the weighing of evidence depends on subjective judgment. Juries disagree. The evidence which has telling force for a juryman who, has himself had experience of the circumstances of the accused may seem much less compulsive to another juryman who has not had that experience. What it was reasonable for me to believe about Venice when I only knew it from pictures is something which it would be quite unreasonable for me to believe now when I have seen the reality. This is why what it is reasonable for a man to believe rests in the last resort on the man he is and the experience he has had.

In Plato's *Phaedo* a friend of Socrates says: 'It is very hard or even impossible to gain certainty about theological questions, but it would be cowardly not to do one's best to examine them. We should take the best theory which human intelligence can supply, and the one most difficult to refute, and take it as a raft on which to sail the seas of life, whatever the danger, unless of course we could make the journey more safely on the barque of a word of God' (p. 85, slightly shortened). I may be told that this safer vessel is available to us in a Divine Revelation, and that the raft of natural theology, or historical criticism, or even philosophy, has outlived its usefulness. If, however, the Divine Revelation is supposed to be contained in the New Testament, I recall that we are there bidden to love God with all our *mind* (διάνοια) as well as with our heart and strength. The Synoptics all include the word 'mind'. Therefore, revelation itself would bid us be true to what we think, to use our minds, to follow, as Plato said, the argument whithersoever it leads. And this is what I have striven to do in this book.

CHAPTER 10

TRANSCENDENCE AND IMMANENCE[1]

Consider Oliver Wendell Holmes's moving hymn:

> Lord of all being, throned afar,
> Thy glory flames from sun and star;
> Centre and soul of every sphere,
> Yet to each loving heart, how near.

Here, if anywhere, is paradox, and it is with this paradox that I am concerned in this chapter. At the end of what I have to say paradox may remain. What remains of the Athanasian Creed is another matter.

That God is transcendent, throned afar, is the belief of Judaism, and, I think, of Islam. It is also Christian doctrine. In fact the notion of transcendence has been carried so far that we are now asked to believe in a *Deus absconditus*, a hidden God, far beyond our ken and understanding. We may be asked to believe more, but I wish first to consider the view that the whole truth about God is that he transcends this world, and even time and space, and that we ought not to think of him otherwise. Certainly this is how he is represented in many of the Psalms, in the Prophets, let alone the Pentateuch, and in many familiar hymns, especially of course those based on the Psalms.

On this view, God is perfect and changeless from everlasting to everlasting yet, at some point in time (how can this be made intelligible?) he created the universe, and, in due course, man. After this creation there are two worlds, the one on which we live, and another, the dwelling-place of the Most High. Owing to man's disobedience, the original goodness of this world has been destroyed. The taint of evil pervades the whole of it; good is unattainable here; to die is gain, and far, far better. Man is born in sin; he cannot help doing wrong; he is cut off from God by his very humanity. The gulf between man and God may be bridged

[1] This chapter elaborates and expands the argument of pages 158 ff. above. It was originally a lecture delivered at St Mary's College, St Andrews, on March 4, 1968. In places there are repetitions of points made in my book, *Action*, and indeed in this volume. But I have not excised them all. 'In case I have not said it before, I will repeat it again' was a pedagogical aphorism of an Irishman who was a successful teacher.

by acceptance of a faith preached by St Paul, but it cannot be destroyed. God is in Heaven, not here, and hither he cannot be brought. It is supposed that we can work out our salvation with fear and trembling by obeying God's law, but the emphasis is on fear and trembling. God is Lord; we humble ourselves before his majesty; he is transcendent, in Heaven and not here.

To this view there are objections. (i) If God is just transcendent, in another world from this, does he ever interfere in this world's affairs, and, if so, how? Transcendentalists have felt the force of this question, especially in connection with prayer. In a period of drought, is it sensible to pray for rain? 'Not a bit of use', said the nineteenth-century Duke (query, of Devonshire), when the Prayer Book collect for rain was read on Sunday, 'not a bit of use, while the wind's in the east'. 'Not a bit of use', say the more sophisticated, because God does nothing here at all. He has set the universe running on fixed lines, which science gradually discovers, and then left it to run itself, save only that free will has been granted to man. It is then maintained that petitionary prayer is misconceived. God, as omnipotent and omniscient, knows already all that we need and desire, and there is no purpose in asking. He will give what is best for us and withhold the rest, whether we ask or not. Prayer is only a recital of the petitioner's psychical state or belief.

There is of course a plain contradiction here, although it is encountered frequently enough. If God has left the universe to run itself, and given man freewill, it is nonsense to say that he knows what men want and will give or withhold it as he knows best. The contradiction is evaded when the gift of freewill is denied. Everything is fore-ordained by God, storms and earthquakes, prayers and sins, Hitler and Albert Schweitzer. Freewill is just a delusion from which men cannot free themselves.

The case for freewill I have argued elsewhere (in my book *Action*). I only point out here that these evasions of petitionary prayer run counter to the teaching and the practice of the moral and religious teacher of our Western civilization. 'Give us this day our daily bread.' 'Father, if thou be willing, remove this cup from me.' (Matthew vi. 8, is followed immediately by the Lord's Prayer. Verse 32 and Luke xii. 30 do not forbid petitionary prayer, but only tell us what petitions to avoid.)

The Transcendentalist may take a different line and hold that God did give man freewill and thereby limited his power of interference in the world's affairs. Prayer will not change God's mind and will, but he does control in the world all for which man's free-will is not responsible. This view finds expression on bills of lading, for example. The shipping and insurance companies take no responsibility for what they call an Act of God. Thus man is responsible for moral evil, and for much physical evil too, but God controls earthquakes, storms, and the like. It is difficult to accept from the Transcendentalist either that God does not interfere, or that he interferes only to cause disasters.

Perhaps the commonest question put to Christians is: 'If God is good, loving, all powerful, omniscient, why does he not stop war and give us universal peace? Even mortal human beings alleviate misery when they can; why does God, looking down from Heaven on to this world, permit so much evil, so much suffering?' The Transcendentalist, like Dean Inge, for example, can only answer: God does not interfere; his purposes are inscrutable; but we must remember that this world is transient, and in the last resort, does not matter. It is only a preparation for life in the other world, where God is, transcending this one.

(ii) A second objection to the Transcendentalist is that his doctrine leads to quietism. On his view, God is changeless. When we are tormented by the ballet of this world's miseries and stupidities and sins, we can turn our backs on it and lift our eyes to God in his eternal splendour far beyond this terrestrial ball. To know more of God we must abstract ourselves from our mortal and fleeting environment, and look elsewhere. Abandon the world; contemplate the eternal verities; by that route alone is it possible to get nearer to God. But if 'be still and know that I am God' is taken as a principle to govern the whole of life and not only a part of it, then it follows that the nearer you get to God the less you do. Goodness is confined to a morality of don'ts. Your business is contemplation, not action; your salvation depends on your being unspotted by contaminaton with this world. This is quietism, and its consequence is that action is sinful. This world is so evil that progress in it can only be infinitesimal and therefore not worth while. For the Transcendentalist the good is in Heaven, perfect, finished, changeless. Attempts to introduce it or to further it in this place of probation are doomed to failure *ab initio*. An austere monasticism is best.

To these objections to the view that God is purely transcendent, and to the inferences which I have drawn from it, there are at least two replies. One is that I have been appealing to reason, and reason is an enemy of faith. The other is mysticism. These two objections seem to me to stand on the same level. Since the eighteenth century, the age of reason, the voice of reason cannot be stilled. To say that God's ways are not our ways, and that they must just be accepted mystically, if they are apprehended at all, and that reverent acceptance, without any rational criticism, ought to be our attitude, is to reduce religion to emotion or intuition, and to deny it its proper place in man's intellectual life. We may grant that emotion is not to be excluded: however else can the continued existence and apparent advance of the Roman Catholic Church be explained? But reason is not to be excluded either. Reason, it is not impious to hold, was given to us for our use and guidance. What faith grasps cannot now exempt itself from rational examination. The great Christian mystics may have had insights which later reflection may have confirmed; other pronouncements of theirs may have lacked this confirmation. They were apt to prefer contemplation to action, instead of uniting the two. They may even have sometimes regarded action as almost sinful; but Jesus went about doing good.

(iii) I quote from Sir James Baillie:[1] 'People often think that, in saying that God is *entirely* beyond our grasp, they are paying him a great compliment and doing him honour. They do not see that, in saying so little of him, they are treating him to condemnation or contempt. That whose highest attribute is beyond our ken is next door to being nothing for us at all'. (In this quotation I have substituted 'God' for 'Absolute' and 'him' for 'it'. I have also italicized 'entirely'.)

Finding this view of the pure transcendence of God unsatisfactory, some have gone to the opposite extreme and espoused a sort of pantheism. On this view, it is a mistake to think of God as far off in Heaven; on the contrary, he is here, immanent in all the world and in every one of us. He is not unreachable by us, but close to the heart and mind of man, closer indeed than hands or feet. This view I call Immanentist, and to it too I have objections to offer. It sems to me to have been characteristic of the Modernist movement of the late nineteenth century and the first quarter of the twentieth. It appears especially in that movement's Christology.

The Modernists dismissed most of the Gospel miracles as inherently improbable. They were prepared to accept the miracles

[1] *Reflections on Life and Religion* (London, 1952), p. 254.

of healing—could they not be readily explained by modern psychology?—but the remainder they jettisoned as victims of scientific and historical criticism. The Virgin Birth is dismissed as a late fiction, and the post-Resurrection appearances are all classed as subjective. The argument is that fact and mode can be separated. The Gospel statements can be rejected, while the doctrines, suitably interpreted, can be retained. For example, the Divinity of Christ can be retained, because divinity is simply perfect humanity. Jesus attained human perfection, and thus was God, the goal of human evolution. Evolution itself was simply the process wherein God is immanent and whereby he makes himself progressively more known. On this view, Jesus might have ceased at any time to be Christ, by just turning a deaf ear to his high calling. He was an ordinary man, with like passions as ourselves, but he did not sin; and in his sinless life of love and peace, divinity was not only revealed but realized. No other view is possible if God is immanent, and if there is no transcendent God to become incarnate in a unique individual.

This view has an implication which scandalized many churchmen when it was plainly stated, as I recall, at the Modern Churchmen's Conference in 1921. If divinity is simply perfect humanity, then we are all 'potential Christs'. It is a far cry from the fact that we are all miserable sinners to the belief that we are potential gods, or potentially God. The distinguished Anglican theologian (Bethune-Baker) who taught that we are all 'potential Christs' had moved some distance from the orthodox belief that Christ was unique and just what we potentially are not.

This modernist Immanentism, however, tries to eat its cake and have it, for it claims (as indeed holders of different views have done) to be Christian while rejecting most of what Christianity has been. There seems to me to be a flaw in its logic. It is very strong on the use of reason, rightly, I think. It accepts the immutability of scientific law as God working immanently in the world. On what ground, then, does it accept the colossal miracle that Jesus—on its own principles an ordinary man—did not sin? Why did the Modernists believe that he was Perfect Man? One of them (H. D. A. Major) said: 'We hold it as an act of faith that he did not sin.' Now, why? For what reason? These Modern Churchmen strained at the gnat of walking on the waves and swallowed the camel of the perfection of a man. I think that Kirsopp Lake was right when he said that if you accept the Modernists' presuppositions and critical methods, you cannot stop where they do. Of course it is argued on the other side that the orthodox doctrine is that Jesus was not just man, but *perfect* man, and that perfect man could still a storm and even raise the dead. Since of perfect man we have no experience, perhaps we would be safer not to speculate on his personality, identity, or powers.

The Modernists used prayers. To whom did they pray? Could it be to the God inside or immanent in themselves? Moreover, if Jesus, an ordinary man, became Christ, and if we are all potential Christs, what would the end of the process be if this potentiality were realized? Would all men become gods, so that the number of gods approached infinity, or would they all be absorbed into an undifferentiated unity, an Absolute whose life, being one without differentiation and therefore without action, would be evacuated of all that makes life worth living? There are some who find attractive an Absolute of this kind, the night wherein all cows are black, as Hegel said, or wherein all cats are grey, as Cervantes said, but this is a curious conclusion for a Christian, however unorthodox, to reach. Much as I sympathize with the Modernists, as the preceding chapters will not have concealed, I cannot believe that their effort to save orthodoxy by re-interpreting it succeeds.

While there is truth in both of the contentions which I have been criticizing, I have tried to show what difficulties arise if transcendence and immanence are each taken abstractly and considered in isolation from one another. Although I have written of 'Transcendentalists' and 'Immanentists', I do not wish to imply that either party necessarily held in abstraction the views that I have criticized. They might claim that they were only emphasizing one of the opposites at the expense of the other, and without denying the validity of the other. I now proceed to take the two opposites together and to try to explain and justify the paradox to which I referred at the start of this chapter.

'Either-Or' was the slogan of Kierkegaard. He rejected Hegel's 'Both-And'. I take my stand with Hegel, and therefore on the doctrine of the unity of opposites. Take any pair of opposites that you please; neither means anything without the other. I go further, neither *is* without the other. When the sun shines, we see the tree and its shadow. They are indissolubly linked. Try to separate infinite and finite, or to keep them apart, and the infinite becomes only another finite, because there is something, the finite, apart from it.

Transcendence and immanence are again a pair of opposites, and we have seen what comes of trying to describe God in the terms of one of them alone. I said at the start that to accept both was paradoxical, but, paradoxical or not, it seems to me to be true. Perhaps I can cast some light on this problem of the unity of opposites if I refer briefly to goodness, and then at greater length to absolute and finite mind.

Consider our moral experience. Is there not a tension within ourselves between what we know we are and yet what we would be. 'Oh! miserable sinner that I am.' And we crave forgiveness. And yet, is not the very consciousness of sin just the faint and flickering candle of the Lord? In so far as we struggle to lead a good life, to *be* good, are we not trying, in our feeble way, to align ourselves with *the* good which transcends us, but which we could never approach if somehow it did not dwell within us? Our failure is our failure to be what we really are ourselves. We are being false, not just to a transcendent judge, but to the infinite goodness which we so imperfectly enshrine. Here, in moral experience, transcendence and immanence unite.

The same is true if we turn from moral experience to mind. Here I will be accused of intellectualism. But the fact remains that man is mind; he can talk; he can distinguish true from false and right from wrong. It is these capacities which make him man and raise him above the beasts. By 'mind' I mean '*Geist*', and I might convey my meaning better if I said 'spirit' instead of 'mind', for that makes clearer the link between man and God, who is Spirit and is to be worshipped in spirit and in truth.

The problem of transcendence and immanence breaks out again as that of the relation between absolute and finite mind or Spirit. As I said in the preceding chapter, the unity of opposites is not difficult to grasp if we think of a curve. It is and must be both concave and convex. It is a curve only because it is the unity of these opposite characteristics. Moreover, neither opposite is intelligible without its counterpart. Concave is meaningless except as contrasted with convex.

Transcendence and immanence seem far more difficult. But I must try to show that here too we cannot have one of the opposites without the other. Reality is their unison and not their separation.

In the first chapter of this book I referred to the well-known passage in which Aristotle argues that 'thought thinks itself by participation in the object of thought; for it becomes an object of thought in coming into contact with and thinking its objects, so that thought and the object of thought are the same. . . . The actuality of thought is life, and God is that actuality'. In quoting this passage, Hegel substituted 'spirit' or 'Absolute Idea' for 'thought' or 'mind', which have overtones which may be too intellectualistic. Spirit he describes as personal and individual, and yet not exclusively so. It is universal, but in its other, the finite, has its own objectivity confronting it. 'All else is error, gloom, opinion, striving, caprice, and transitoriness.'[1] These things exist, in the sense that a mirage exists; but just as a mirage is less real than an oasis, so all else is less real than the real reality of spirit.

Spirit, like thought, has its appropriate opposite, for example, flesh, matter, and letter; but, like thought again, it is not intelligible except in unity with its opposite. This is the problem of transcendence and immanence, infinite and finite. It is also the problem presented to us by consciousness. Consider not its occurence in organisms, but its gradual growth by self-transcendence until it becomes what we can call man's mind. There we reach reality. Nature exists, but it is called and known as nature only because it exists *for* mind. The whole process of nature culminates, by self-transcendence, in mind, or call it 'spirit' if you will.

But the question presses, if reality is finally and at last mind or spirit, whose mind or whose spirit or whose thought are we concerned with? If what Hegel called the Absolute is mind, with what mind have we to do? Who can penetrate the mind of God? And yet, if by his development man rises to the level of mind or spirit, what is his relation to the Absolute, infinite spirit? Man, it has been said, and I have quoted this before, is the candle of the Lord. How is this to be understood? To some it will seem to be an impiety to raise questions like this. 'Canst thou by searching find out God?' (Job xi. 7). But there is higher authority for 'Thou shalt love the Lord thy God with all thy *mind*', as I mentioned in the preceding chapter.

Consequently, I make so bold as to approach the mystery of transcendence and immanence *via* a consideration of absolute and finite mind, of infinite and finite thinking.

It seems obvious to say that, whereas my thought is limited, partial, and finite, the thought of God is infinite. Men's minds are finite, and God's alone is infinite. And yet the attempt to describe a relationship between minds so conceived must break down.

[1] *Science of Logic*, *Werke*[1], v, pp. 327–8.

If the finite and the infinite are set over against one another, so that what is one is *eo ipso* not the other, then each limits or sets bounds to the other. Infinity cannot lie alongside or outside the finite, or otherwise the infinite will cease to be the infinite; it will be bounded by the finite. It will not set limits to itself, but will be limited by something outside itself. Once admit that there can be something outside the infinite, then the latter disappears and only finites remain. The attempt to sever infinite from finite, and set one over against the other, seems to destroy the infinite. But there is an alternative, if finite and infinite are first supposed to be mutually exclusive. The finite can be absorbed into the infinite; outside the infinite there is nothing; the finite is only a logical conception, the negation of the infinite, and that is nothingness. This has seemed to some to be the end of Spinoza's philosophy, just as the result of Leibniz's had seemed to be a plurality of finites.

Start with a cleavage between absolute mind on the one hand, and finite mind on the other, and you must end with either Spinoza or Leibniz, an infinite into which everything finite is dissolved, or a plurality of finites held together by the miracle of Leibniz's pre-established harmony.

Instead of Kierkegaard's Either-Or, we must accept Hegel's Both-And. The infinite and the finite must be inseparable, but both real. Mind, or thought, must be not either infinite or finite, but both. The question that I posed above: Whose thought? suggests an individualism which cannot be true of thought itself. Of thought no one has the monopoly. It is no one's private property, but as public as the air we breathe.

That thought is both infinite and finite is implied in the very character of our own consciousness. The individual is conscious of himself as part of the world of nature, as one amongst other finite objects. There was a time when he did not exist, and there will be a time when he will not be here. He is conscious of himself as limited in space, in time, in intellectual power, in moral achievement.

And yet this cannot be the whole truth. To be conscious of a limit is already to have transcended it. A limit is a boundary between two things; to know one of them as a boundary is to know that something lies beyond. Man is conscious of himself as limited in time only because time exists *for* his consciousness; he can think about it, and therefore can contemplate it *ab extra*. No doubt man is conscious of himself as an object, finite indeed, amongst other finite objects; and yet it is for *mind* that objects are objects. It is mind which makes them so. This is why man is conscious of himself not just as nature, but as spirit too; nature is meaningless except by contrast with, and in connection with, spirit, its opposite. In man nature has risen, so to speak, to consciousness of itself, and in this process it is transcended. Nature, become conscious of itself, is spirit, the only ultimate and final reality. A shadow, error, moral evil, these are all in one sense real, but only in one sense. The thought that has gone astray, the good that has not been done, the shadow which is not the reality, all these are negative, and in that sense are just not what they ought to be, and yet they are intelligible only by reference to the true reality which they have failed, and yet not utterly failed, to enshrine. A false judgment is still a judgment. A man called evil is a moral agent, and to that extent good. He is not just a venomous snake.

It is this compresence of infinite and finite which it is so difficult to understand. The infinite actualizes itself only in the finite which it overreaches and in which it is, however, imperfectly, expressed. 'Man's reach must exceed his grasp, or what's a Heaven for?' is the expression of the tension in man between the ideal and a real achievement, between infinite destiny and finite actuality.

It may seem impious to say that the infinite actualizes itself 'only' in the finite. But Hegel argued that the world is necesssry to God, because, if God is love, his nature cannot be actualized without the creation of objects to love. This may be unorthodox doctrine, but Hegel's view that the finite is a moment *necessarily* within the infinite (for otherwise the infinite is a bare abstraction, 'the nights where all cows are black') should be taken seriously. As Bosanquet said,[1] 'the hardest of all lessons in interpretation is to believe that great men mean what they say'. I think that Hegel was a great man, and here I believe what he says. Professor Paton thinks that this is 'reckless', but I cannot help it. He has also suggested to me that, in claiming *knowledge* of the infinite, Hegel goes too far, because this is beyond our human powers. But it seems to me that if we can *think* of the infinite at all, we must go on to give some content to this conception, or draw out its implications. And in so far as this is what Hegel has done, I cannot but follow him, even if this be lacking in caution.

Our ideas are fluid, vague, shifting, indeterminate until we give

[1] In the Preface to his translation of the *Introduction to Hegel's Philosophy of Fine Art* (London, 1905), p. xix.

them finite form in speaking or writing. They may elude full expression in words, and we change the words in the continual endeavour to give better, fuller, more precise reality to our thought. Perfect expression eludes us; the solution of one problem gives rise to another. The phraseology of the past, imbued with meaning then, is now but dry formalism. (This is the difficulty that credal affirmations cannot evade.) The slogan which inspired men in battle in years gone by may well have lost its magic now, and yet the principle for which men fought had to be embodied in a slogan. Ideals have to be embodied in institutions if they are ever to be operative; and yet the embodiment is ever inadequate, and it has to be changed, lest it ossify. The infinite actualizes itself in and through the finite.

Man is conscious of himself not only as nature but as spirit too, because in man nature has risen to self-consciousness. The history of man, and of the individual, is the process of self-transcendence, the gradual rise of man from natural beginnings to a consciousness of a spiritual destiny, realized in part by the development of mind from feeling,[1] or all that man shares with animals, to self-consciousness. The process is one of negation; thinking is both infinite and finite. It rejects its finite expressions only because they conflict with its potential yet unactualized infinity. Draft after draft may be destroyed, and even the one retained at last is recognized to be unsatisfactory. No finite draft will satisfy the infinity of mind. This is the human predicament.

This is why achievement does not satisfy. Life is the enduring possession of the infinite, and the endless, and therefore finite, quest for its actualization and expression.

By contemplating his own death, as he has to do, man nevertheless rises above it. In a sense, in virtue of his mind, he transcends his immediate finitude, and can rise, as spirit, above his finite existence. As part of nature, man dies; and yet since he can think of this fact, he can rise above the time series and can become conscious of himself as spirit. 'As in Adam all die, so in Christ shall all be made alive.' For Adam there is a cleavage between man, the finite, and God, the transcendent. But this abstract analysis of differences within a unity is itself superseded by the doctrine of the indwelling of the Holy Spirit.

A difficulty arises because we tend to emphasize our individu-

[1] Of this development I have given an account in the early chapters of my book *Action* (London, 1968).

ality, our separation from one another, for separation is finitude, and we might find ourselves back with Leibniz's monads. It is true that our bodies are juxtaposed in space. But space is a way of thinking necessarily associated with objects; it is something which mind thinks, not something in which mind is. The truth of the plurality of men is their unity, though not uniformity, in God. The spirit is one, transcendent and immanent, absolute and finite.

The corollaries of this doctrine will not commend themselves to those for whom individuality is the supreme category. We may speak of the 'unique' value of the individual or the person, but this must not blind us to certain facts. It is not in the experience of our self-enclosed individuality or personality that we discover what we value most or find most real. In love and friendship the barriers of individuality give way before the sharing of a mutual experience, an experience which remains a duality, and which yet presupposes and points towards a unity which makes it what it is. In thought, two minds are at one. When you and I think the same thought, our minds, our selves, are identical in a sense in which we are not if we wear clothes of the same colour and design, or merely utter the same words. The advance to mutual understanding lies through transcending our personal or individual point of view until we reach 'common ground'.

In art, in religion, in thoughtful investigation, it is when we are, as we say, 'taken out of ourselves' that our experience is most real and most valued. This is the advance beyond individuality to that in which individuality is grounded. 'Our hearts are restless until they find rest in Thee.'

The one relation out of which no thought or category can be forced is its relation to its opposite, i.e. its own appropriate opposite. Love is not opposed to the many, nor hatred to the one. Unity is opposed to plurality, but, given unity of a certain kind, the plurality is of the same kind. Thus I distinguish my body from other bodies, and my personality from other personalities.

My personality is my consciousness of myself as a person related to and distinct from other persons, but this plurality implies a unity as its proper opposite, a unity in which this purality is grounded. The ground cannot itself be merely a personality, or even an infinite personality, for that is a contradiction in terms. To speak of a personal God is to use a metaphor, though one which we cannot evade.

In trying to elucidate the mysterious unity of transcendence and immanence, of infinite and finite, I have been drawing, not only on Hegel, but also on Greek philosophy, especially on Book x of Plato's *Laws* and Book Λ of Aristotle's *Metaphysics*. But I have been thinking too of the language which St Paul used to the Athenians, when he spoke of God as he in whom we live and move and have our being (Acts xvii. 28). It also seems to me that this attempt to combine the transcendent and the immanent, God the Father and God the indwelling Spirit, is also an attempt to follow the religion of Jesus, or at least that part of it in which he transcends Judaism, that part of it which speaks more directly to the hearts of some of us than the religion which St Paul and others made out of him.

INDEX

GEORGE ALLEN & UNWIN LTD

Head Office
40 Museum Street, London, W.C.1
Telephone: 01–405 8577

Sales, Distribution and Accounts Departments
Park Lane, Hemel Hempstead, Herts.
Telephone: 0442 3244

Athens: 34 Panepistimiou Street
Auckland: P.O. Box 36013, Northcote Central N.4
Barbados: P.O. Box 222, Bridgetown
Beirut: Deeb Building, Jeanne d'Arc Street
Bombay: 103-105 Fort Street, Bombay 1
Buenos Aires: Escritorio 454-459, Florida 165
Calcutta: 285J Bepin Behari Ganguli Street, Calcutta 12
Cape Town: 68 Shortmarket Street
Hong Kong: 105 Wing On Mansion, 26 Hancow Road, Kowloon
Ibadan: P.O. Box 62
Karachi: Karachi Chambers, Mcleod Road
Madras: 2/18 Mount Road, Madras
Mexico: Villalongin 32, Mexico 5, D.F.
Nairobi: P.O. Box 30583
Philippines: P.O. Box 157, Quezon City D-502
Rio de Janeiro: Caixa Postal 2537-Zc-00
Singapore: 36c Prinsep Street, Singapore 7
Sydney N.S.W.: Bradbury House, 55 York Street
Tokyo: C.P.O. Box 1728, Tokyo 100-91
Toronto: 81 Curlew Drive, Don Mills

Recent Titles in the Muirhead Library of Philosophy Series

LOUIS ARNAUD REID

Meaning in the Arts

In this book the author of the influential *A Study in Aesthetics* (1931) explores in a new way the crucial problem of aesthetic meaning. Art lovers naturally assume that works of art are in some sense meaningful. But is 'meaning' in an art such as poetry the same *kind* of meaning as in another, say dance or pure music? Again, if there is meaning *in* art, can the meaning *of* a work be stated clearly in words? If it can, the making of the work was unnecessary; if not, then how can it mean anything? One answer has been 'through "expression" '. Art may be expressive, certainly; it springs from the human situation. But if art in some sense expresses, it also transmutes, discovering new, created, autonomous meaning, inseparably embodied in the presented material forms of, art, and known only through vital participation in which body and imaginative mind are working together.

The thesis of embodiment (rather than expression) as a key idea is worked and tested out in different arts. In the process, most of the seminal topics of aesthetics are lucidly discussed—the language of criticism, 'expression', aesthetic 'surface', representative and 'abstract' arts (with special attention to musical meaning), feeling and emotion, symbols and the 'embodiment-symbol', knowledge, truth, 'revelation'. The last part of the book is an eloquent plea for the development, in every liberal education, of insight into the arts as a unique form of *knowledge*.

MICHAEL WHITEMAN

Philosophy of Space of Time

A mathematician who is also a mystic is exceptionally well qualified to survey the mysterious subject of space and time. Dr. Whiteman, Associate Professor of Applied Mathematics at Cape Town University and author of *The Mystical Life*, brings the mathematician's detachment and the mystic's insight to this book and presents the most thorough treatment of space and time yet seen. For the expert he provides an indispensable textbook likely to stand unchallenged for many years; for the intelligent layman, an opening into an absorbing field of knowledge, in a world where religious beliefs about the nature of the universe have lost their authority, but interest in the infinite is at its greatest.

MORRIS LAZEROWITZ

Philosophy and Illusion

The main object of this book of essays, as of its two predecessors, is to improve our understanding of technical philosophy. The central enigma of philosophy, which has caused deep disquiet in many thinking people, is that nothing in it ever gets settled; rival philosophical views and their arguments remain suspended in thin air, without finding a secure resting place. The essays may be considered as contributions toward answering a question raised by Hans Reichenbach: 'Why must philosophers forego a generally accepted philosophy?' The explanatory hypothesis that the author puts forward about the peculiar linguistic character of philosophical views and arguments will be recognized as having its roots in Ludwig Wittgenstein's later thought. Some readers of Wittgenstein distinguish between the 'false philosophy' in his work and other parts of it which they find more congenial to their own thinking. Wittgenstein's 'false philosophy' falls into what Professor Lazerowitz calls 'Metaphilosophy' and it holds out promise of an enlightening answer to Reichenbach's question. The essays of this book have the unity of a single orientation, the development of a hypothesis which will give us insight into the workings of philosophy. A number of basic issues are treated in the light of this hypothesis; issues centring on empiricism and rationalism, direct and indirect perception, the reality of time, induction, the existence of propositions, causation, the reality of relations.

H. H. PRICE

Belief

This volume is based on the two series of Gifford Lectures delivered at the University of Aberdeen in 1959–60, though a good deal of new material has been added since. The first part begins with a discussion of the relation between belief and knowledge and of the various sorts of evidence we have for our beliefs, including the evidence of testimony.

In the second part we turn to the modern 'dispositional analysis', and two different versions of this are considered. The conclusions reached are then applied to several important but puzzling topics, for instance half-belief and the relation between belief 'in' and belief 'that'. The last third of this volume is concerned with moral and religious beliefs.

H. D. LEWIS

The Elusive Mind

We are apt in many ways to think of ourselves entirely in terms of our bodies. But we seem also to be more than our bodies. What is this more, or is that a misleading question? Professor Lewis, in sharp opposition to prevailing views in philosophy today, boldly maintains that mental processes are of a quite different nature from physical ones and belong to an entity which is elusive in the sense that it can only be known, in the first instance, by each person in his own case in the course of having any kind of experience. This 'elusive' self is much involved with the body in any conditions we know, but it could also survive the dissolution of the body. In presenting these views, the author offers us the substance of the First Series of Gifford Lectures he delivered in the University of Edinburgh; and, in what he says on such topics as dreaming, mysticism, and the 'I-Thou' relation and on Christian theology, he gives us a glimpse of the Second Series which will appear in due course as a separate work.

In the present book the views of important contemporary thinkers, including Ryle, Hampshire, Malcolm, Feigl and Ayer, are subjected to an exceptionally close and critical scrutiny.

Translated by A. V. MILLER

Hegel's Science of Logic

With the current revival of interest in Hegel there is a real need for an accurate and faithful presentation of this fundamentally important work. It is hoped that the present translation, which has taken the author several years to complete, will fill this need and will attract not only the professional student but also the philosophically minded layman who has neglected Hegel because of the alleged difficulties of his terminology and style. These difficulties should not be a serious obstacle to one who is prepared to approach the *Science of Logic* objectively and to make the effort to grasp what Hegel has to say; his exposition is, in fact, lucid. When Hegel wrote the *Logic* he knew just what to say and how to say it precisely. The difficulties encountered by the student arise mainly from his inability to think dialectically—the only method, Hegel insists, appropriate to a genuine philosophical enquiry. Those who wish to learn what Hegel really taught, what he really accomplished as a thinker, will not shrink from making the strenuous effort to learn this method. They will find their perseverance richly rewarded. The Hegelian *Notion*—Hegel's unique contribution to philosophy—can be comprehended only by those who think dialectically.

LONDON: GEORGE ALLEN AND UNWIN LTD